# HOTSPOTS
# COSTA
## COSTA DE ALMERIA

**Written by Teresa Fisher, updated by Katherine Rushton**

**Published by Thomas Cook Publishing**
A division of Thomas Cook Tour Operations Limited.
Company registration no. 1450464 England
The Thomas Cook Business Park, Unit 9, Coningsby Road,
Peterborough PE3 8SB, United Kingdom
Email: sales@thomascook.com, Tel: + 44 (0) 1733 416477
www.thomascookpublishing.com

**Produced by Cambridge Publishing Management Limited**
Burr Elm Court, Main Street, Caldecote CB23 7NU

ISBN: 978-1-84157-853-8

**First edition © 2006 Thomas Cook Publishing**
This second edition © 2008
Text © Thomas Cook Publishing,
Maps © Thomas Cook Publishing/PC Graphics (UK) Limited

Series Editor: Diane Ashmore
Production/DTP: Steven Collins

Printed and bound in Spain by GraphyCems

Cover photography by SIME/Giovanni Simeone

# CONTENTS

## WHAT'S IN YOUR GUIDEBOOK?

**Independent authors** Impartial, up-to-date information from our travel experts who meticulously source local knowledge.

**Experience** Thomas Cook's 165 years in the travel industry and guidebook publishing enriches every word with expertise you can trust.

**Travel know-how** Contributions by thousands of staff around the globe, each one living and breathing travel.

**Editors** Travel-publishing professionals, pulling everything together to craft a perfect blend of words, pictures, maps and design.

**You, the traveller** We deliver a practical, no-nonsense approach to information, geared to how you really use it.

● *The sun-drenched Costa del Sol*

# INTRODUCTION
Getting to know the Costa del Sol
& Costa de Almería

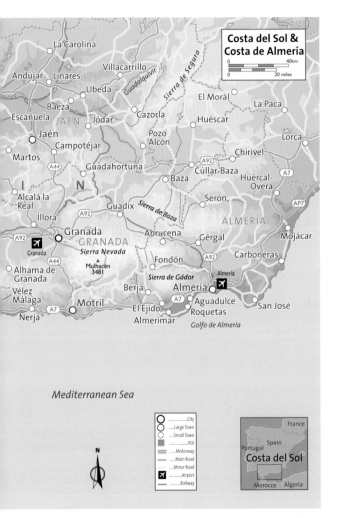

Costa del Sol &
Costa de Almería

0          40km
0     20 miles

La Carolina

Villacarrillo
Andújar  Linares
                    Guadalquivir        Sierra de Segura
          Úbeda                          El Moral        La Paca
    Baeza
Escañuela  JAÉN   Jódar    Cazorla    Huéscar
    Jaén                   Pozo                              Lorca
        Campotéjar         Alcón
Martos                                Chirivel
        (A44)    Guadahortuna      (A92)                    Huércal-
                                    Cúllar-Baza             Overa      (A7)
    I        N                                                        (AP7)
                          Baza              Serón
Alcalá la                                           ALMERÍA
Real    Guadix   Sierra de Baza
    Íllora                                                    Mojácar
(A92)    Granada        Abrucena   Gérgal
        GRANADA                                Carboneras
Granada  Sierra Nevada
(A44)       Mulhacén    Fondón      (A92)
            3481       Sierra de Gádor    Almería
Alhama de              Berja              Almería
Granada                          (A7)  Aguadulce        San José
Vélez                El Ejido  Roquetas
Málaga   Motril     Almerimar   Golfo de Almería
    (A7)
Nerja

Mediterranean Sea

○  .............City
○  .......Large Town
○  .......Small Town
■  .................POI
▬▬  ...........Motorway
▬▬  .........Main Road
▬▬  .........Minor Road
✈  ..............Airport
▬▬  .............Railway

N
⊕

                    France
        Spain
Portugal
    Costa del Sol
    Morocco  Algeria

7

# Getting to know the Costa del Sol & Costa de Almería

The sun-drenched coastline, from Gibraltar in the west to Mojácar in the east, is one of the most popular holiday playgrounds in Europe, and one that caters for all tastes with its sandy beaches, world-class golfing facilities, and lively bars and restaurants.

On the Costa del Sol, the highly developed resorts of Torremolinos, Benalmádena and Fuengirola have become synonymous with a buzzing expat nightlife and simple beach fun, while the more upmarket ports of Marbella and Puerto Banús are filled with chichi restaurants and celebrity-studded bars. Inland, the *pueblos blancos* (white towns) of Nerja and Mijas cater well to tourists, but still manage to retain their rustic charm and offer a glimpse of old-fashioned Andalucía.

Heading east of Nerja along the Costa de Almería, the land is largely devoted to intensive horticulture. The resorts dotted in between are less busy and built up than on the Costa del Sol, and offer a sleepy haven to tourists seeking a quiet beach getaway.

## ANDALUCÍA

On a typical day, you might get up late and spend your time sunbathing, swimming, eating and drinking, with a lazy siesta to occupy the greater part of the afternoon. But what if you get tired of lying on the beach all day? Then, take time to explore the rest of the famous and fascinating Andalucía region – the land of bullfighting, flamenco and sherry. Over the years, various invaders have left their mark on the countryside, including the Moors, who ruled the region for seven centuries and named it al-Andalus. The enchanting *pueblos blancos* (white towns) dotted about the countryside date from this period, as do many of the treasures of the principal cities, Córdoba and Granada, and Sevilla, the vibrant capital of Andalucía.

This region of sleepy, whitewashed villages, historical cities and stunning landscapes (ranging from some of the highest mountains in Spain to seemingly endless sandy beaches) is also the spirited and vibrant land of country fiestas, electrifying nightlife, flamenco shows and distinctive cuisine. The variety and spirit of Andalucía, combined with all the fun of a beach-resort holiday, is what draws millions of visitors from all over the world to make southern Spain Europe's number-one holiday destination.

🔺 *Andalucia is full of romantic, whitewashed villages*

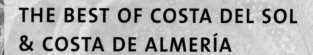

# THE BEST OF COSTA DEL SOL & COSTA DE ALMERÍA

Southern Spain's coastal region offers so much more than just beaches.

## TOP 10 ATTRACTIONS

- **The Caves of Nerja** With their spectacular rock formations and prehistoric paintings (see page 46).

- **Córdoba** Especially La Mezquita (The Great Mosque), one of the finest Moorish buildings in the world (see page 77).

- **Granada** Home of the Alhambra Palace – known as the eighth wonder of the world – and its refreshing Generalife Gardens (see page 84).

- **Marbella's Casco Antiguo, or Old Town** With its picturesque main square, the Plaza de los Naranjos (see page 25).

- **Las Alpujarras** A wonderful area for hill walking or mountain biking, famed for its *jamón serrano* (see page 92).

- **Mojácar** Idyllic *pueblo blanco* – a hilltop village with a gorgeous beach nearby (see page 88).

- **Puerto Banús** Andalucía's most sophisticated marina with its luxury yachts, trendy shops, restaurants and bars (see page 21).

- **Ronda** With its famous bullring, ancient bridge and amazing setting high above the Guadalevín river (see page 66).

- **Barter for local produce and handicrafts at** Fuengirola's Tuesday market – the biggest and best market on the coast (see page 32).

- **Join a boat excursion** to explore the coastline and to visit neighbouring resorts, or go on a dolphin safari (see page 31).

● *The intricate beauty of the Dome of the Mihrab, Córdoba*

## SYMBOLS KEY

The following symbols are used throughout this book:

ⓐ address  ⓣ telephone  ⓦ website address  ⓔ email
ⓛ opening times  ⓘ important

The following symbols are used on the maps:

| | | | |
|---|---|---|---|
| 🄸 information office | | ⭕ | city |
| ✉ post office | | ⭕ | large town |
| 🄰 shopping | | ○ | small town |
| ✈ airport | | ■ | POI (point of interest) |
| ➕ hospital | | ▬ | motorway |
| ⏻ police station | | — | main road |
| 🚍 bus station | | — | minor road |
| 🚆 railway station | | — | railway |
| ✝ church | | | |

❶ numbers denote featured cafés, restaurants & evening venues

### RESTAURANT CATEGORIES

The symbol after the name of each restaurant listed in this guide indicates the price of a typical three-course meal without drinks for one person:

£ under €12   ££ €12–45   £££ more than €45

❿ *The region has delightful small coves and beautiful beaches*

The marina at Estepona

# Estepona

The beachfront resort of Estepona is quietly becoming one of the most fashionable places on the western Costas. Its pleasure marina is making glamorous Puerto Banús look to its laurels, while its golf courses attract many well-known international faces. Estepona, though, caters better for young families than the jet set. It makes no sightseeing demands on visitors, but there are few more relaxing places for a stroll than its tidy, palm-lined esplanades. For a drink and a good meal, head for the cafés and restaurants around the jasmine-scented Plaza de las Flores.

This modest, low-rise town spreads along a large expanse of beach. Its economic mainstays once revolved around fishing and citrus growing – the streets in the old quarter all have charming, ceramic name plaques decorated with lemons. Unlike some parts of the Costas, agriculture and fishing have not entirely given way to the demands of tourism, and the town still has an unpretentious and refreshingly Spanish air. Estepona's harbour is a hive of activity when the night's catch is landed on the quaysides. If you get up very early, the fish market by the Puerto Pesquero is a sight to see, but it's mostly over by 07.00. The quiet, flattish coastline is guarded by ancient fortresses, some dating from Roman or Phoenician times. Some distance inland, the road through the Serranía Bermeja climbs through forests where a unique species of fir tree called the *pinsapo* flourishes. From the Refugio de los Reales *mirador* (viewing point), spectacular views extend as far as Gibraltar.

## BEACHES

Estepona manages a 21-km (13-mile) stretch of coastline, and proudly waves a Blue Flag (the EU's quality stamp) on several of its beaches. The main strand is the long, sandy **Playa de la Rada**, punctuated by *chiringuitos* (beach bars) and the wooden watchtowers of the lifeguards. **Playa del Cristo**, near the marina, is a delightful oyster-shaped cove of sheltered, gently shelving sand, ideal for children. If you prefer life in the buff, head eastwards for the **Costa Natura**, Spain's oldest naturist resort.

## THINGS TO SEE & DO

### Golf

Estepona has five local golf courses and several championship links around the smart *urbanisación* of Sotogrande. The superb **Valderrama** course rose to fame when it hosted the Ryder Cup in 1997.
ⓐ 11310 Sotogrande ⓣ 956 79 12 00 ⓦ www.valderrama.com

### Polo

For polo, head for Sotogrande, near Estepona, where British and Argentinian teams practise their chukkas during the winter, on Spain's only permanent polo field. Tuition available. ⓐ Santa María Polo
ⓣ 956 61 00 12/61 01 32 ⓦ www.santamariapoloclub.com

### Selwo

A successful safari park with over 2,000 exotic species, from giraffes to panthers, in their natural habitat. There are also daily shows.
ⓐ Carretera N340, Km 162.5 ⓣ 902 19 04 82 ⓦ www.selwo.es
ⓘ Admission charge ⓛ 10.00–18.00 Mon–Sun

## TAKING A BREAK

**La Gamba £** Simple seafood tapas bar, with fish and some meats.
ⓐ Calle Terraza 25 ⓣ 952 80 56 07 ⓛ Closed Thur and 15 Feb–15 Mar

**Gelateria Caffe del Centro £** Coffee, sandwiches and delicious Italian ice creams served in a pretty square with a fountain. ⓐ Plaza Doctor 1
ⓣ 952 80 55 96 ⓛ 11.00–03.00

**Chiringuito Rossi ££** This family-friendly *chiringuito* (beach bar) is suitable for a quick snack or a full-blown meal. Great beach views all the way to Gibraltar. ⓐ Paseo Maritimo, opposite Plaza Ortiz ⓣ 952 11 32 99
ⓛ Mar–Oct

● *A fishing boat returning to Estepona*

**Meson Casa Orta ££** Lively tapas bar serving traditional Spanish hams and cheeses, as well as *montaditos* (traditional little sandwiches). ⓐ Calle Rocio Jurado 15 ❶ 952 80 44 38 ● Closed Tues

## AFTER DARK

### Restaurants
**Casa de Mi Abuela ££** Rustic decor and hearty platters of chargrilled meat. ⓐ Calle Caridad 54 ❶ 952 79 19 67 ● Closed Tues and May

**El Rincon Toscano ££** Smart Italian restaurant with wide variety of fish, meat and pasta dishes. ⓐ Calle Real 22–26 ❶ 952 79 59 14 ● Closed Wed, and Feb and Nov

**Marisqueíra El Galiván del Mar £££** Great seafood restaurant in one of the old town's prettiest plazas. ⓐ Plaza Doctor Arce ❶ 952 80 28 56 ● Closed Tues, and Mon in winter

# San Pedro de Alcántara

West of Marbella, the little town of San Pedro nestles on a broad strip of fertile, coastal lowland sheltered by rugged hills. It is less well known than its glitzy neighbours, but Costa del Sol experts recognise a good thing when they see it. Many expatriates have chosen to settle here, giving the place a more permanent, residential feel than some of the holiday resorts, and its stylish interior-design boutiques and smart little restaurants are well patronized. All around, large, elegant private villas lie masked behind walls and subtropical gardens – if you're sharp-eyed enough, you may spot some famous faces.

San Pedro dates from the 1860s, when it was established as a model farming community with an agricultural training school. Today many of its country estates are prosperous tourist enclaves or golf courses. Much of the town lies inland behind the coastal highway, and it's a fair step down to the beach. There's less nightlife here than in Marbella or Puerto Banús, but its plus points include a well-managed stretch of quiet, clean seafront and three of the most interesting archaeological remains anywhere on the coast. The neatly kept old town centres on the shady Avenida Marqués del Duero, lined with enticing shops and cafés, orange trees and fountains. Behind, on Plaza de la Iglesia, twin palm trees frame the white facade of San Pedro's charming parish church.

## BEACHES

There are fantastic watersports facilities at **Bora-Bora Beach**, including waterskiing, motorboats, canoes, rowboats, as well as scuba diving.
❸ Urb. Lindavista, Calle Gitanilla

## THINGS TO SEE & DO

### Archaeological remains
Behind the beach at Las Bovedas lies a Roman bath house with a wood-fired heating system, and a 4th-century basilica with a beautiful

font. Four kilometres (2½ miles) east at Río Verde is a Roman villa decorated with delightful mosaics showing kitchen utensils.
🕿 952 78 13 60 🕘 Free guided tours on Tues, Thur and Sat at noon. Meet at the tourist office inside the archway which signposts entry into San Pedro and Marbella, on the Carretera N340, Km 170.5 (no transport provided, but you may be able to get a lift)

## Cable skiing

Waterskiing with a difference; you're towed along a fixed overhead wire – easier than an erratic, fast-moving boat. Perfect your skills on a calm inland lake. **Cable Ski Marbella** ⓐ Parque de las Medranas 🕿 952 78 55 79 ⓦ www.cableskimarbella.com 🕘 11.00–15.00 and 16.00–21.00

## Riding

Call a day ahead to book an hour's trek through the countryside with one of the instructors, at **Lakeview Equestrian Centre**.
ⓐ Urbanisacion Valle del Sol 🕿 952 78 69 34 🕘 Tues–Sun

## TAKING A BREAK

**La Pesquera de San Pedro ££** Enjoy sardines barbecued on the seafront or prawns 'pil pil' (in sizzling oil with garlic and chilli) at the local branch of this chain of high quality fish restaurants ⓐ Avenida del Mediterraneo, Playa San Pedro de Alcántara 🕿 952 78 77 21

### SHOPPING
**Street Market** Every Thursday there's a lively market near the Sports Pavilion, for those with an eye for a bargain.
**Vassiliki** This is a popular backwater for local artists. For postcards, pottery, jewellery, ceramics and unique examples of local art, head for the shop called Katoi. ⓐ On the Ponti Road, next door to Mythos Taverna 🕿 264 50 31 700

● *San Pedro's pretty church*

**La Jaralera £££** Small family-run restaurant serving classic Spanish dishes, expertly cooked. The veal chops are great. ⓐ Calle Velez Malaga 3 ① 952 78 91 95 ⓛ 13.00–16.00 and 20.00–24.00; closed Mon

## AFTER DARK

**Restaurants**
**Caruso ££** Smart, modern restaurant serving popular dishes and adventurous daily specials. ⓐ Calle Andalucía, Local 6 ① 952 78 22 93 ⓛ Dinner only, 19.30–24.00 Mon–Sat

**El Gamonal ££** Some of the best cooking around, in a flower-filled, country setting off the Ronda road. Roast specialities. ⓐ Camino La Quinta ① 952 78 99 21 ⓛ Closed Wed and mid-Jan–mid-Feb

**Mesón El Coto £££** Lovely terrace restaurant high in the hills on the road to Ronda. Attentive service and excellent country dishes and game. ⓐ Urbanisacion el Madroñal, Carretera de Ronda ① 952 78 66 88 ⓛ 19.30–00.30

# Puerto Banús

Marbella's exclusive and world famous marina – Puerto Banús – just a short distance to the west, is the playground of the rich and famous, where the international jet set come to shop, socialize and party. It is the Costa del Sol's most celebrated port, filled with a dazzling collection of massive, ostentatious yachts and gin palaces operated by battalions of uniformed crew – very much the place to see and be seen. Behind the port, the 'Golden Mile' to Marbella throbs with nightspots and restaurants. Spot King Fahd's exotic Arabian palace, Mar Mar. Inland, the glitterati villas and exclusive country clubs of Nueva Andalucía stretch back into the hills.

This glamorous complex, named after its designer José Banús, was created in 1968, and its success has spawned a number of rival wannabes up and down the coast. Few, though, can boast the spectacular backdrop of rugged hills, which gives the marina its photogenic setting. A village-like development of eye-catching, pantiled apartments in Spanish and Moorish styles surrounds the waterfront walkways, forming a seamless chain of eating places, bars and boutiques. As the sun sinks below the yardarm, beautiful people strut their stuff on the quaysides before leisurely making their way to the most fashionable nightlife venues.

## THINGS TO SEE & DO

### Aquarium Puerto Banús
A fascinating place for all the family, this aquarium is housed in an old watchtower at the port. Displays include sharks, stingrays and octopuses.
ⓐ Torre de control ⓣ 952 81 87 67 ⓛ 10.00–13.30, 16.30–19.30 Mon–Sat

### Golf
No dedicated golfer should miss out on a visit to the **Marbella Golf and Country Club** (see page 25).

## AFTER DARK

### Restaurants

**Azul Marino ££** Superb international fish cuisine served in a smart nautical decor in a magnificent prime waterfront location. ⓐ Muelle Ribera ⓣ 952 81 10 44 ⓦ www.buenas-mesas.com ⓛ 12.00–01.00

**Dalli's Pizza and Pasta Factory ££** Pizza and pasta combined in this cheap and cheerful Italian restaurant, with an adjoining café. ⓐ Avda Fontanilla ⓣ 952 81 86 23 ⓛ 19.00–01.00

**El Rancho del Puerto ££** Suckling pig and other tasty meats in traditional Spanish and international styles are on offer in this steakhouse. ⓐ Muelle Benabola 4 ⓣ 952 81 62 52

**Red Pepper ££** Friendly Greek restaurant right on the quayside. ⓐ Muelle Ribera ⓣ 952 81 21 48 ⓛ 11.00–01.00

**Finca Besaya £££** This exclusive, relaxing hideaway is situated in an old avocado farm nestled high in the hills. Accomplished cooking. ⓐ Urb. Río Verde Alto ⓣ 952 86 13 86 ⓛ 19.30–24.00 Tues–Sun ⓘ Booking essential; dress smartly

**Restaurante Antonio £££** Elegant corner restaurant specialising in seafood, but also offering an extensive selection of delicious meat dishes. ⓐ Muelle Ribera 21 ⓣ 952 81 35 36

### Nightlife

**Cines Gran Marbella ££** English-language films are shown in this seven-screen complex. ⓐ Paseo de la Ribera ⓣ 952 81 00 77 ⓦ www.cinesgranmarbella.com

**Stereo Lounge ££** Modern, chilled out bar with comfy sofas and a marina view ⓐ Muelle Ribera

**Casino £££** Bring plenty of cash for an evening here! ⓐ Hotel H10 Andalucía Plaza ⓣ 952 81 40 00 ⓛ Slot machines from 16.00 hours; casino 19.00–05.00 ❶ Dress smartly and bring your passport

**Olivia Valére £££** Celebrated nightclub, and haunt of the rich and famous. Smart restaurant, sushi and piano bars. ⓐ Carretera de Istán, Km 0.8, Nueva Andalucía ⓣ 952 82 88 61 ⓛ Restaurant 21.00–01.00; nightclub 24.00–05.00

**Sinatra Bar £££** Rub shoulders with the likes of Antonio Banderas in this laid-back, see-and-be-seen, waterfront bar. ⓐ Muelle Ribera 2

## SHOPPING
**Boutique 007** Shop here for the latest in beach and club wear. ⓐ Muelle Ribera 4 ⓣ 952 81 13 95

**La Cañada** Enormous out-of-town shopping mall signposted off the N340 to Marbella, with multi-screen cinema and all the major Spanish high street stores. ⓛ 10.00–22.00 Mon–Sat

**El Corte Inglés** This massive department store and supermarket stocks just about everything! ⓐ Ramón Areces, Centro Comercial Costa Marbella, on the outskirts of Puerto Banús ⓣ 952 90 99 90 ⓦ www.elcorteingles.es ⓛ Closed Sun (winter)

**Craft market** Ideal place to browse for jewellery, bohemian beach-wear and objets d'art, under white tents in the main square.

**Kosas** Embroidery specialists here will personalize a T-shirt for you while you wait. ⓐ Muelle Ribera J5

**Market** A large flea market. ⓐ Held around the bullring of Nueva Andalucía. ⓛ 09.00–14.00 Sat

**Neck & Neck** Posh, children's clothes in a street behind the waterfront. ⓐ Muelle Ribera 10A ⓣ 952 81 48 41

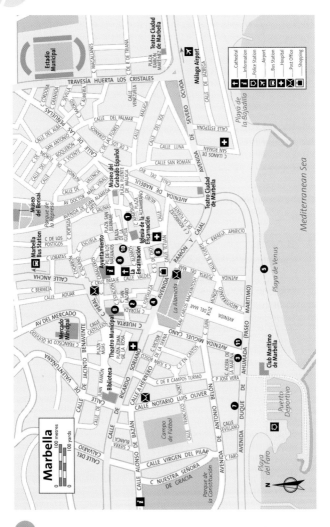

# Marbella

Glamorous and cosmopolitan yet fiercely traditional, Marbella perfectly blends old with new and is considered by many to be the jewel of the resorts along the Costa del Sol.

The old town (*Casco Antiguo*) has been carefully and sympathetically maintained – a quaint pedestrian district of tiny squares and whitewashed houses smothered in bougainvillea clusters round the postcard-pretty Plaza de los Naranjos, named after its orange trees. By contrast, modern Marbella centres around its designer boutique-lined Avenida Ricardo de Soviano, and the seafront. In the evenings, its smart promenade becomes a catwalk for well-dressed Spanish families.

## BEACHES & WATERSPORTS

The Marbella coastline has 26 km (16 miles) of attractive, well-tended sandy beaches. The central beaches stretch either side of the *puerto deportivo* (yacht marina) below elegant, traffic-free promenades. There are plenty of places to lounge beneath a parasol, but many visitors seize the opportunity to enjoy energetic, high-tech watersports of all kinds.

**Club Maritimo de Marbella** Scuba-diving, sailing and windsurfing near Marbella's yacht harbour. ⓐ Puerto Deportivo ⓣ 952 77 25 04

**Happy Divers Marbella** Scuba-diving and boat trips. ⓐ Puerto Deportivo ⓣ 952 88 90 00 ⓦ www.happy-divers-marbella.com

**Hotel Marbella Club** Motorboats, windsurfing, kitesurfing, waterskiing, pedalos, canoes and catamarans.
ⓐ Blvd Principe Alfonso von Hohenlohe ⓣ 952 82 22 11

**Hotel Puente Romano** Motorboats, windsurfing, kitesurfing, waterskiing, pedalos, canoes and catamarans. ⓐ Carretera N340, Km 177 ⓣ 952 82 09 00 (mobile) ⓦ www.puenteromano.com

## THINGS TO SEE & DO

### Funny Beach

Go-karting, laser games, water-slides, bumper boats (an aquatic version of dodgems), mini-golf, jetskiing and a giant Scalextric.

ⓐ Carretera N340, Km 184 ❶ 952 82 33 59 Ⓦ www.funnybeach.net

### Golf

For anyone interested in golf there are many splendid courses in the area immediately around Marbella. So high is the standard of the golfing facilities that numerous top international players come here to practise during the winter, and some have permanent connections with the area. The swankiest clubs are situated mostly to the west in the hills of Nueva Andalucía. Most demand a handicap certificate, and require booking well in advance. Contact the tourist office for details.

**Aloha Golf** ⓐ Nueva Andalucía Ⓦ www.clubdegolfaloha.com

**Las Brisas** Ⓦ www.brisasgolf.com

**Marbella Golf and Country Club** This exclusive course is on the Málaga side ⓐ Carretera N340, Km 188 ❶ 952 83 05 00 Ⓦ www.marbellagolf.com

**La Quinta** Ⓦ www.laquintagolf.com

### Museo del Bonsai (Bonsai Museum)

The only such venture in Spain, with 300 specimens up to 450 years old, set in attractive Japanese-style gardens.

ⓐ Parque Arroyo de la Represa ❶ 952 86 29 26 ❶ 10.30–13.30, 17.00–20.00 (summer) and 10.30–13.30, 16.00–19.00 (winter) ❶ Admission charge

### Museo del Grabado Español Contemporáneo
### (Museum of Contemporary Spanish Engravings)

Important collection of engravings in a former 17th-century hospital near the Arab city walls. It provides a comprehensive overview of Spanish artistic trends since the 19th century, including works by Picasso, Miró and Dalí.

ⓐ Calle Hospital Bazán ❶ 952 71 57 41 ❶ 10.00–13.45, 19.00–21.00 Tues–Sat (summer); 10.00–14.00, 17.30–20.30 (winter) ❶ Admission charge

### Teatro Ciudad de Marbella (City Theatre)

A plush venue that attracts an impressive rosta of international operas, concerts and dance shows, as well as plays in Spanish. Ticket prices can be very reasonable.

ⓐ Plaza Ramón Martinez ❶ 952 90 31 59 ❶ Famous names also perform at the grander hotels

## EXCURSIONS
### Mini cruise

Travel by boat from Marbella to Puerto Banús. The journey takes approximately 30 minutes.

ⓐ Victoria S, Marbella Marina ❶ 952 45 67 50 🕓 Departures from Marbella at regular intervals ❶ Dolphin-watching trips are also available

### Ojén

This picturesque mountain village lies about 10 km (6 miles) north of Marbella, high in the hills of the Sierra Blanca. Just beyond the village, in a forested game reserve, is the Refugio de Juanar, a charming hunting-lodge inn (❶ 952 88 10 00 🌐 www.juanar.com). This makes a good starting point for walks through the hills, where you may catch sight of the rare Iberian ibex, a horned goat-like creature. If you don't feel energetic, just enjoy a good lunch. Ojén is on a bus route from Marbella. Jeep excursions, treks and mountain bike hire are organised by **Monte Aventura**. Ask your rep, hotel or the tourist office for more information.

ⓐ Oficina de Turismo Rural, Plaza de Andalucía 1, Ojén ❶ 952 88 15 19 🌐 www.monteaventura.com

## TAKING A BREAK

**Bar Altamirano £** ❶  Characterful spot on a quiet square near the walls at the back of the old town. Tiled wall-plaques promise exotic sea fare: bleaks, saurels, elephant fish. ⓐ Plaza de Altamirano ❶ 952 82 49 32 🕓 13.00–16.00, 20.00–24.00. Closed Wed

**El Estrecho £** ❷  A real locals' tapas bar down a narrow alleyway.
ⓐ Calle San Lázaro 12 ❶ 952 77 00 04 ❶ Mon–Sat

**Bar el Bodegon ££** ❸  Choose from 80 varieties of *montaditos*
(traditional little sandwiches) to enjoy sitting at barrels overlooking the
marina. ⓐ Paseo Maritimo

**Cafetería Marbella ££** ❹  A good bet for breakfast or coffee on Marbella's
smartest shopping street, near the shady Alameda Gardens. Plenty of
terrace space. ⓐ Avenida Ramón y Cajal ❶ 952 86 11 44

## AFTER DARK

### Restaurants
**Palms £** ❺  Beach café specializing in more interesting salads
than most, as well as excellent catch-of-the-day fish dishes.
ⓐ Playa de Venus

**El Patio Andaluz £** ❻  A simple but good value Spanish restaurant set in
a pleasant, cool, flower-filled courtyard. ⓐ Calle San Juan de Dios 4

**Restaurante la Axarquía £** ❼  Good value fish restaurant specialising in
paella and whole fish baked in salt. ⓐ Paseo Maritimo ❶ 952 86 36 31
❶ Closed Wed

**Mena ££** ❽  The terrace restaurants on the main square are geared
towards tourists, but this little place isn't bad value. Lovely setting in an
old house with tables under the orange trees. ⓐ 10 Plaza de los Naranjos
❶ 952 77 15 97 ❶ 11.00–23.00 Mon–Sat

**La Pesquera ££** ❾  Highly rated seafood chain with traditional Spanish
decor and good *dorado* (red mullet) and lobster. ⓐ Plaza de la Victoria or
Paseo Maritimo ❶ 952 76 51 70/86 85 20 ❿ www.lapesquera.com

**SHOPPING**

Marbella's smartest shopping street is **Ramón y Cajal**. The old town has lots of crafts and attractive souvenirs on sale. Marbella's street market takes place by the football stadium on Mondays.

**Bravo** One of Marbella's best leatherware shops – bags and shoes galore. ⓐ Ramón y Cajal 5 ⓣ 952 77 32 35

**El Camino** Traditional flamenco costumes and accessories for children and adults. ⓐ Calle Estación 2 ⓣ 952 77 50 04

**Málaga Plaza** Shopping complex with a range of boutiques on several floors and a café. ⓐ Armengual de la Mota 12
ⓣ 952 61 40 40

**Restaurante Buenaventura Plaza £££** ❿ A restaurant for a special occasion, strung with fairy lights and situated off a pretty little square in the old town. The inventive menu offers modern takes on traditional Spanish dishes, like lobster with mushroom jam or duck with Malaga wine. ⓐ Plaza de la Iglesia de la Encarnación 5 ⓣ 952 85 80 69

**Santiago £££** ⓫ A suave but rather expensive seafront restaurant situated near the port. On offer is a splendid array of authentic Andalucían dishes served in a lively and very Spanish atmosphere.
ⓐ Paseo Marítimo 5 ⓣ 952 77 00 78 ⓦ www.restaurantesantiago.com

**Nightlife**

Most of Marbella's liveliest nightlife centres on Puerto Banús (see pages 22–3), or takes place in various hotels. Dress up, refuel your wallet and head for the cocktail bars of the **Marbella Club** or the **Puente Romano** or to Marbella's chichi Moroccan-themed garden club, **La Notte** (ⓐ Camino de la Cruz ⓣ 952 77 76 25 ⓛ Closed Sun). There are a few bars around Puerto Deportivo, but for some real action head to **Dreamers**, a popular club that hosts visiting DJs and stays open to 06.00 or 07.00 at weekends. ⓐ Carretera Cádiz Km 175 ⓣ 952 81 20 80

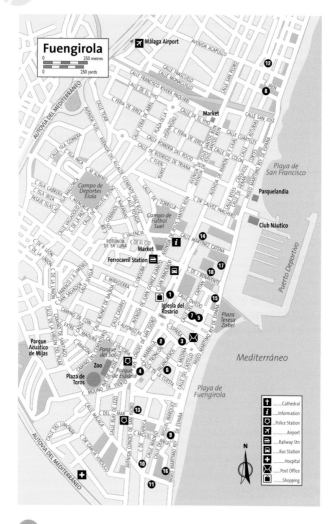

**Fuengirola**

Málaga Airport

| | |
|---|---|
| ✝ | ....Cathedral |
| i | ....Information |
| 🛡 | ...Police Station |
| ✈ | ....Airport |
| 🚆 | ....Railway Stn |
| 🚌 | ....Bus Station |
| ✚ | ....Hospital |
| ✉ | ....Post Office |
| 🛍 | ....Shopping |

Playa de San Francisco

Parquelandia

Club Náutico

Puerto Deportivo

Mediterráneo

Parque Acuático de Mijas

Zoo

Plaza de Toros

Parque de España

Playa de Fuengirola

N

# Fuengirola

Fuengirola is a lively and popular seaside resort with beautiful beaches, a vibrant nightlife and lots of attractions for all ages. The beach is the centre of activity–day and night. It is lined by one of the longest promenades on the Mediterranean (it takes about two hours to walk from one end to the other). Just behind the palm-lined walkway, the old fishermen's district of Santa Fé has retained its Andalucían character. Its narrow, whitewashed streets contain some of the best restaurants in town, especially around the main square – Plaza de la Constitución – and along Calle Moncayo, nicknamed the 'Street of the Hungry'.

## BEACHES

Fuengirola boasts one of the best seafronts of the entire Costa, with over 7 km (4½ miles) of clean, sandy beaches, divided into restaurant-beach strips, each renting out lounge chairs, parasols and pedalos. The central beaches of Santa Amalia, Castillo and Fuengirola lap the old town to either side of the port, while to the east the sand continues in an unending sweep past the hotel zones of Los Boliches and Torreblanca.

## THINGS TO SEE & DO

### Boat trips
Daily fishing trips, dolphin-spotting and sunset cruises are all on offer at the marina.
**The Dawn Approach** ☏ 649 19 41 03 ⓦ www.dawnapproach.co.uk
**Joren Maria II** ☏ 952 44 48 81

### Fuengirola Zoo
First-class zoo with a simulated rainforest and more than 140 animal species. ⓐ Avda Camilo Jose Cela 6 ☏ 952 66 63 01 ⓛ 10.00–20.00, or 24.00 in high season ❶ Admission charge

## Parque Acuático de Mijas

Children will love the waterslides, rapids and surf pools at this refreshing water park, just ten minutes by bus from Fuengirola bus station.
ⓐ Carretera N340, Km 209 ⓣ 952 46 04 04 ⓦ www.aquamijas.com
ⓛ From 10.00, Apr–Oct ⓘ Admission charge

## Parquelandia

Swings, slides, a trampoline, a bouncy castle, and mini-karting on the seafront.
ⓐ Puerto Deportivo, Paseo Marítimo ⓣ 952 58 12 86

## TAKING A BREAK

**As Garnichas £** ❶   Informal tapas bar popular with locals, serving great octopus salad and prawns 'pil pil'. ⓐ Calle Larga 4 ⓣ 952 19 72 22
ⓛ 11.00–24.00 Mon–Sun

**Café Fresco £** ❷   Excellent English-run restaurant with tasty soups, extensive salad bar, wraps, sandwiches and fresh, mixed juices like carrot, orange and ginger. ⓐ Las Rampas ⓣ 635 86 37 95

**Cafetería Costa del Sol £** ❸   The place to enjoy breakfast Spanish-style – *churros* dipped into a cup of thick, sticky hot chocolate. A great cure for a hangover! ⓐ Calle Marbella 3 ⓣ 952 47 17 09

### SHOPPING

Shopping in Fuengirola ranges from cheap souvenir shops to high-class boutiques. For the best bargains, visit the **Tuesday morning market** – the largest and most colourful market on the Costa del Sol. ⓐ Avenida Jesús Santos Rein ⓛ 10.00–15.00. Or try **Centro Comercial Parque Miramar**, a modern shopping centre.
ⓐ Avenida de la Encarnacion

## AFTER DARK

### Restaurants

**Meson Galán £** ❹ Deliciously tender *solomillo* (sirloin) and other meaty tapas, along with inexpensive wine that can be enjoyed inside or at barrels on the pavement. ⓐ Calle Marbella 13 ❶ 952 46 64 34 ⓛ Closed Sun

**O Mamma Mia £** ❺ Popular, family-orientated Italian restaurant with quick, friendly service. Good value for money. ⓐ Calle de la Cruz 23 ❶ 952 47 32 51

**Monopol ££** ❻ Rustic decor, informal atmosphere and unusual, international meats, from 'Zurich veal' to 'Madagascan beef'. ⓐ Calle Palangreros 7 ❶ 952 47 44 48 ⓛ Open dinner only, closed Sun and mid-July–mid-Aug

🔺 *The main focus of most people's holidays is bound to be the beach*

**Moochers ££** ❼ English-owned restaurant in the town centre with a roof terrace. Irish beef, seafood, crepes and vegetarian specials, often with a jazz accompaniment. ⓐ Calle de la Cruz 17 ❶ 952 47 71 54 🕒 19.00–01.00 ❗ Booking is recommended

**Namaste India ££** ❽ Fuengirola's top Indian restaurant. ⓐ Calle Jaen (opposite Hotel Angela) ❶ 952 46 74 10 🕒 12.00 to late

**Old Swiss House ££** ❾ *Rösti* and fondue, but plenty else too in this pleasant restaurant. ⓐ Marina Nacional 28, one block behind the beach ❶ 952 47 26 06 🕒 13.00–15.30, 19.00–24.00; closed Tues

**Restaurante Misono ££** ❿ Authentic Japanese 'teppenyaki steakhouse' where meat is cooked at the table on sizzling hot plates. Delicious tempura and sushi are also served, making the lacklustre decor forgivable. ⓐ Corner of Calle Madrid and Héroes de Baler ❶ 952 46 49 32 🕒 14.00–16.00, 20.00–24.00 Tues–Sun

**El Sultán ££** ⓫ Moroccan specialities in a lavish, Alhambra-like setting. Belly dancing at weekends. ⓐ Héroes de Baler ❶ 952 46 20 78 🕒 3.00–15.45, 19.30–23.45, closed Mon

**La Langosta £££** ⓬ Long-established restaurant specializing in lobster, as its name suggests. Mussels in saffron, sole in champagne and beef goulash are other favourites. ⓐ Lape de Vega ❶ 952 47 50 49 🕒 19.00–24.00 Mon–Sat

### Nightlife

Hidden away opposite the Old Town Café and down some steps to the harbour is a long row of friendly and inexpensive bars mostly run by expats. Two good bets are English-run **JJ's** (❶ 952 58 82 33) and **The Family Bar** (❶ 952 46 16 41) a Dutch-run bar and restaurant that hosts live music every night from 20.30. On the front line of bars overlooking the harbour, the German **Ku'Damm Berlin** (ⓐ Puerto Deportivo 12

🕓 952 47 28 64) bar and restaurant is another popular venue that serves good food and regularly hosts live music.

**The Cotton Club ££** ⑬ Chilled-out atmosphere, the pick of the bunch. Live music most Thursdays. ⓐ Avenida Condes de San Isidro 9

**Linekers ££** ⑭ This UK sports bar and fun pub, belonging to Gary's brother Wayne, has cheap beer (happy hour 17.00–19.00), pool tables, English DJs, karaoke and theme nights. ⓐ Puerto Deportivo, Club Náutico 🕓 952 47 62 85 Ⓦ www.linekers-bar.com

**Mai Tai ££** ⑮ From 20.00 to midnight is 'Strictly Ballroom' (foxtrot, tango, salsa) then midnight to 07.00 is 'Strictly Clubbing' (soul, disco, rock and house). ⓐ Paseo Marítimo, near Hotel El Puerto ❶ Admission charge

**Ministry ££** ⑯ A welcome break from the euro pop standard, this nightclub is a hit, and often features top names from the international DJs circuit, though it has no connection with London's Ministry of Sound. ⓐ Paseo Marítimo Ⓛ 23.00–dawn Wed–Sat (happy hour 24.00–04.00) ❶ Free entry except at weekends

**Old Town Café ££** ⑰ A small bar with rustic decor, popular with young Spanish. ⓐ Paseo Marítimo 🕓 952 58 07 39 Ⓦ www.oldtown-cafe.com

**Video Café ££** ⑱ If clubbing is not your scene but you like to let your hair down, come here after 21.00 for a wild night of cocktails and karaoke. ⓐ Avenida Jacinto Benavente 🕓 952 47 18 66 Ⓛ 10.00–02.00 Mon–Sat (happy hour 20.00–22.00)

# Benalmádena Costa

Benalmádena Costa is a lively, purpose-built holiday resort with a wide variety of entertainment for all the family, good watersports facilities, shops, bars and restaurants appealing to all tastes and budgets. The stunning tiered marina greatly enhances the resort's appeal, and its many bars and nightclubs have made Benalmádena one of southern Spain's hottest nightspots.

Benalmádena is made up of three different districts. Cosmopolitan Benalmádena Costa is the main tourist centre and is focused around three main areas of entertainment – Bonanza Square, 24-Hour Square and the Marina – together offering any number of things to see and do.

Further inland, tucked into the foothills of the Sierra de Mijas, Benalmádena Pueblo is the old part of town – the original Andalucían white village, still full of rural charm. Its sleepy, narrow streets and twisting alleyways of white-painted houses with terracotta-tiled roofs present a complete contrast to the hectic pace of the coastal strip. The main square, Plaza de España, contains the statue that has become the symbol of Benalmádena – a young girl offering water in an upturned shell.

Midway between the Pueblo and the coastline lies the main residential district, called Arroyo de la Miel (meaning 'stream of honey'). It is a busy, fashionable area with hundreds of apartment blocks and many popular restaurants, bars and clubs. Tivoli World, the resort's top children's attraction, is here, and on Fridays the local market provides a good opportunity to buy cheap provisions and local handicrafts.

## BEACHES

Benalmádena boasts 9 km (5½ miles) of beaches to the west of the new marina – some sandy, some shingle, some artificial – but they are all clean and safe for swimming (**Playa Santa Ana** even has a European Blue Flag for cleanliness). **Playa Las Yucas**, between Hotel Torrequebrada and Hotel Costa Azul, is a nudist beach.

## THINGS TO SEE & DO

### Auditorio de Benalmádena (Benalmádena Auditorium)

Enjoy theatre, music and dance at the town's grand auditorium located next to the Parque de la Paloma. Events run throughout the year, including a festival at the end of July.

ⓐ Avenida Antonio Marchada ① 952 44 06 40

### Boat trips

Take a boat to see dolphins or go on an organised mini-cruise. Some boat companies combine the trip with a visit to the Sea Life aquarium and a mini-train ride at a special rate. Ask your holiday representative for details.

### Castillo Bil-Bil

You'll spot this eye-catching crenellated Moorish building in bright reddish-pink towards the western end of the seafront. Formerly a private house, it has been converted into a gallery for temporary exhibitions. It is decorated with tiles and Arabic bas-reliefs.

ⓐ Avda Antonio Machado 78 ① 952 44 43 20 ⓒ 10.00–13.00, 15.00–20.00 ① Admission charge

🔺 *Puerto Deportivo*

## Golf

Benalmádena's challenging 18-hole **Torrequebrada Golf Course** (not far from town in the hills), is reputed to be a 'thinking person's course'.
ⓐ Carretera N340, Km 220 Urb. Torrequebrada ❶ 952 44 27 42

## Horse trekking

Trekking in the hills on a half-day guided excursion, ending with a barbecue back at the riding school. There's a restaurant and children's play area too. **Club Hípico de Benalmádena**.
ⓐ Finca Villa Vieja, Urb. Torrequebrada Norte ❶ 952 56 84 84
ⓦ www.clubhipico.com

## Motomercado

Explore the region by bike or scooter.
ⓐ Avenida de Alay ❶ 952 44 11 31 ⓦ www.rentabike.org

## Museo de Cultura Precolombina (Pre-Columbus Museum)

Charming little museum in the old village with an interesting collection of pre-Conquest South American artefacts and local antiquities.
ⓐ Avenida Juan Luis Peralta 49 ❶ 952 44 85 93 ⓦ www.sealife.es
🕒 09.30–13.30, 18.00–20.00 Tues–Sat (summer); 17.00–19.00 (winter)
❶ Admission charge

## Puerto Deportivo

Looking more like a giant wedding cake than a marina, the Puerto Deportivo complex, with its countless open air bars, restaurants and clubs, really comes to life at night. There is even underwater lighting.

## Sea Life Acuario (Aquarium)

A small but excellent aquarium with walk-through water-tunnel, touch-tanks, and feeding demonstrations.
ⓐ Puerto Deportivo ❶ 952 56 01 50 🕒 10.00–midnight
❶ Admission charge

**SHOPPING**

**Andycraft** Ethnic imports from Southeast Asia. 🅐 Dársena de Levante, Local 7, Puerto Deportivo 🕿 952 57 41 53

**La Artesanía Española** Spanish handicrafts, including ceramics, candles and olive wood. 🅐 12 Avda Antonio Machado

**Artesanía Piel** Interesting leather goods. 🅐 Puerto Deportivo

**La Maison en Fleur** Souvenirs and presents, including tasteful flower bouquets in silk and paper. 🅐 Dársena de Levante, Local Puerto Deportivo A12 🕿 952 56 02 99

### Selwo Marina

Aquatic wildlife park housing dolphins, penguins and sea lions, as well as a 3D cinema and snake house.

🅐 Parque de Paloma, Benalmadena 🕿 952 19 04 82 🕒 Closed mid-Dec–mid-Feb 🛈 Admission charge

### Teleférico (Cable-car)

A 15-minute ride to the mountain summit, from where you can walk down.

🅐 Arroyo de la Miel, near Tivoli 🕿 952 57 50 38 🕒 10.30–01.00 (summer); 10.30–21.30 (winter).

### Tivoli World

Theme park with world-class rides, Wild West entertainment, and flamenco shows.

🅐 Arroyo de la Miel 🕿 952 57 70 16 🕸 www.tivoli.es

🕒 Eves May–Sept, until 02.00 in high season; restricted hours Sept–Apr

🛈 Entrance fee for children under 1 m (3 ft)

## TAKING A BREAK

**Café Fresco £** Just like its sister-establishment in Fuengirola, this English-run café sells excellent soups, salads, wraps and zingy fruit and veg smoothies. 🅐 Avenida de la Constitution 17 🕿 618 82 68 26

**Club de Buceo Los Delfines £** The popular little canteen attached to the diving school by the harbour offers unpretentious, perfectly fresh fish and good tapas. There are tables outside, and friendly service. Excellent value. ⓐ Puerto Deportivo ⓣ 952 44 42 13 ⓛ 13.00–16.30, 20.30–24.00 for food, 08.00–24.00 for drinks

**Metro £** Inexpensive pizzas, pastas and ice creams, served indoors or on a terrace overlooking the port. ⓐ Puerto Marina ⓣ 952 44 64 60

## AFTER DARK

### Restaurants
**El Elefante £** Wholesome English home cooking accompanied by various raucous entertainments seven nights a week, including cabaret and hypnotists. ⓐ Benalmádena Plaza ⓣ 952 56 22 46 ⓛ 20.00–01.00

**Raffles ££** Friendly English-run restaurant serving good quality English fare, set near the station opposite a pretty church. ⓐ Plaza de la Iglesia 1 ⓣ 952 56 78 74 ⓛ 11.00–22.00, closed Sat

**Restaurante Carretero Puerto ££** Pleasant Spanish fish restaurant with all the traditional dishes, as well as slightly more unusual ones like razor clams and seafood casserole. ⓐ Pueblo Marinero, local E3-4 ⓣ 952 56 41 90 ⓛ 13.00–17.00, 20.00–24.00

**Ristorante Pinocho ££** Mid-range Italian with three types of lasagne and good pizzas and ice creams, or you can cross the street to the Cafeteria y Heladeria Pinocho instead. ⓐ Puerto Marina ⓐ 952 44 08 92

**Mar de Alboran £££** One of the smartest restaurants in town, near the entrance to the port, offering accomplished modern cooking with a decent wine list. A menu of the day gives you a chance to sample the chef's best efforts. ⓐ Avenida de Alay 5 ⓣ 952 44 64 27 ⓛ Closed Sun eve and Mon (winter); closed Sun eve (summer)

**El Mero £££** Sophisticated fish restaurant with a cool terrace overhanging the port. Try the bream baked in salt. ⓐ Dársena de Levante, Puerto Marina ❶ 952 44 07 52 ❷ 13.00–01.00

**Ventorillo de la Perra £££** A very typical Spanish restaurant. Both local Malagueño cooking and general Spanish fare. ⓐ Avenida Constitución 115, Arroyo de la Miel ❶ 952 44 19 66 ❷ 13.00–15.00, 19.30–23.30 Tues–Sun

### Nightlife

**Bar Maracas ££** Samba the night away at this buzzing nightspot. Arrive before midnight as queues can be long. Be warned – dancing on the bar top is a regular occurence. ⓐ Puerto Deportivo

**Casino Torrequebrada ££** Take your passport and try your luck at the tables. Not quite as smart as Marbella, but do dress up. ⓐ Avenida del Sol ❶ 952 44 60 00 ❷ 21.00–05.00

**Joy ££** A popular club in the Marina area, attracting locals and visitors alike. ⓐ Puerto Marina ❶ 952 56 34 44 ❷ 23.00–06.00 ❶ Admission charge; Thursday is ladies' night (free entry)

**Kiu ££** One of the biggest discos in town, with three DJs and three dance floors, all playing different types of music. ⓐ Plaza Solymar (just off 24-Hour Square) ❶ 952 44 05 18 ❷ 23.00–06.30 (until 07.30 Fri and Sat) ❶ Admission charge

**Sala de Fiestas Fortuna £££** Hotel Torrequebrada's cabaret act is a spectacular show. ⓐ Avenida del Sol ❶ 952 44 60 00 ❷ 10.30–00.30 Tues–Sat ❶ Admission charge includes dinner and entry to the casino

⬢ *Torremolinos is a world-famous resort*

# Torremolinos

The tourist boom of the 1950s, which made the Costa del Sol a world-famous holiday destination, all began in Torremolinos – a tiny fishing village turned big, brash resort. Few places in southern Spain can offer as many hotels, bars and discos and, for sun-worshippers, 'Torrie' offers some of the best beaches on the coast.

It once had a reputation for being a downmarket resort, but recently it has shaken off this 'Terrible Torrie' image by smartening up the town and building an elegant beach promenade. By night, the neon-lit streets of the attractive old town throng with life until the early hours.

**La Carihuela** (the westernmost district of the resort) is a reminder of Torrie's humble beginnings as a simple fishing village. Its atmospheric, whitewashed streets are crammed with restaurants, and fishermen still barbecue silvery sardines on wooden skewers on the beach.

## BEACHES

You can find some of the best beaches of the Costa here, notably the two main beaches of **Playamar** and **Bajondillo**. Then there is **Playa de la Carihuela** fringing Torrie's original fishing village to the west, and the quieter **Playa de los Alamos** to the east. All have sunbeds, umbrellas and pedalos to rent, as well as showers, café-bars and restaurants. At the height of summer, there are often beach volleyball and football competitions. Watersports are available at nearby Benalmádena marina.

## THINGS TO SEE & DO

### Aquapark

Largest waterpark in Europe, with wave machines, a 'water mountain', and 30 water-slides.

ⓐ Carretera de Circunvalacíon 10 (near Palacio de Congresos)

ⓣ 952 38 88 88 ⓛ 10.00–18.00 (May, June, Sept); 10.00–19.00 (Jul–Aug)

ⓘ Admission charge

### Crocodile Park

Nature park dedicated to 300 crocs, including the largest specimen in Europe.

ⓐ Calle Ciba 14 ❶ 952 05 17 82 ⓦ www.crocodile-park.com
🕒 10.00–19.00 (July–Sept); 10.00–17.00 (Oct–Apr) ❶ Admission charge

### El Ranchito

If you are unable to get to Jerez to see the dancing horses, come here to this similar but smaller show.

ⓐ Senda del Pilar 4 ❶ 952 38 31 40 ❶ Dressage demonstrations each Wed at 17.45 – book through your hotel

## AFTER DARK

### Restaurants

**La Alcena** £ Small but tasty menu of simply-cooked meat and fish.
ⓐ Doña Maria Barrabino 11 ❶ 952 38 72 02 🕒 Closed Sun

**Pepe Carmen** £ Paella is the speciality at this friendly, beachside café-restaurant. ⓐ Playa Camino Los Alamos ❶ 952 37 46 95

**Restaurant Chino Sanda** £ Cheap, cheerful Chinese restaurant.
ⓐ Avenida Lido 6, Nuevo Playamar ❶ 952 38 09 40 🕒 12.00–16.30, 18.30–24.00

**Restaurante Nuevo Playamar** £ Just next to 'Bar el Guíri' (the Englishman's bar) is a restaurant that is the complete opposite – very Spanish. Delicious and reasonably priced fried fish is served either as a main course or as tapas to a mostly local crowd. ⓐ Avenida del Lido 10 ❶ 952 37 16 75 🕒 Closed Sat

**Restaurante Casa Paco las Carihuela** ££ Established in 1969, this ever-popular fish restaurant is one of the best in the area and has a buzzing atmosphere to boot. ⓐ Paseo Maritimo de la Carihuela ❶ 952 05 13 81 🕒 Closed Mon

**Frutos £££** A great place for spotting celebrities. ⓐ Carretera N340, Km 228 ☎ 952 38 14 50 🕒 Closed Sun eve

A bewildering number of bars and restaurants line La Carihuela's long seafront. Some of the best include **Casa Guaquin** (🕒 closed Mon) and its neighbour **El Roqueo** (🕒 closed Tues), at Calle Carmen 35 and 37. **Casa Juan** (☎ 952 38 56 56) and **La Jábega** (☎ 952 38 63 75) are both on Calle del Mar at 14 and 17

### Nightlife

**Palladium £** Regularly packed solid with visitors dancing to the latest rave sounds. ⓐ Avenida Palma de Mallorca 36 ☎ 952 38 42 89 🕒 23.00–06.00 ❶ Admission charge

**Eugenios ££** A long-established disco in 'Torrole', one of the last remaining clubs in the Pueblo Blanco area. ⓐ Calle Case Blanca 22 ☎ 952 38 11 31

**El Luga ££** If dancing's not your thing, try karaoke until the early hours. ⓐ Avenida Manantiales 6 ☎ 952 37 54 26

**Veronia ££** Music ranges from Sevillanas to the latest chart toppers at this lively night club near the centre of town. ⓐ Avenida Salvador Allende 10 ☎ 952 37 24 70 🕒 23.00–late

# Nerja

Nerja (pronounced 'nair-ha') is the jewel of the eastern Costa del Sol. Its tranquil, whitewashed streets and typical Andalucían houses, adorned with splashy scarlet geraniums in terracotta pots, retain much of its ancient Moorish character as well as offering visitors fabulous beaches and all the facilities of an international resort. The old town is centred on the Balcón de Europa – all the cobbled streets and alleyways radiate outward from here, full of cafés and tiny boutiques. By night they are twinkling with fairy lights and alive with tapas bars and restaurants.

## BEACHES

**Playa Calahonda**, a fishermen's beach, and **Playa El Salón** are nearest to the town. **Playa Torrecilla** to the west is larger and less crowded, but the best beach is **Playa Burriana** (20 minutes' walk on the coastal footpath to the east) with excellent facilities, lively bars and restaurants. **Club Náutique Nerja** has details of diving, sailing, mountain biking, riding and guided walks. ⓐ Avenida Castilla Pérez 2 ⓣ 952 52 46 54

## THINGS TO SEE & DO

### Balcón de Europa (Balcony of Europe)
This magnificent, palm-lined promenade sits atop a cliff, providing dazzling views. It marks the start of a scenic path that winds its way over the rocks bordering the shore to Burriana Beach. Horse and carriage tours also leave from here, taking in most of Nerja's sights.

### Cuevas de Nerja (Caves of Nerja)
One of the most visited sights in Spain – vast prehistoric caverns of magically lit stalactites and stalagmites. One cave, containing Stone Age paintings and the largest stalactite in the world, has been dubbed the 'Cathedral of the Costa del Sol'.
ⓐ Carretera de Maro ⓣ 952 52 95 20 ⓛ 10.00–14.00, 16.00–18.30

## SHOPPING

Every Tuesday morning, the streets of Nerja come alive for the weekly market – worth a stop, as are these:

**Creaciones Guacamayo** Costume jewellery in a kaleidoscopic range of semiprecious stones. ⓐ Calle El Barrio 4 ⓣ 952 52 15 30

**Licorería Arce** Wines, spirits, liqueurs and tobacco products. ⓐ Calle Pintada 7 ⓣ 952 52 81 21 ⓔ licoreriaarce@Nerja.net

**Manos** Handmade leatherware, jewellery, pottery and other goodies. ⓐ Calle Pintada ⓣ 952 52 11 37/8 ⓛ Mon–Sat

## EXCURSIONS

### Almuñecar

A popular destination with Spaniards from the Granada area. The outskirts are rather built up, but it has a few interesting sights (such as Roman and Phoenician remains), good, if greyish, beaches and lots of lively bars and restaurants. Make for the old town around the Plaza Ayuntamiento for good tapas. From the coastal highway, a picturesque mountain road winds its way through the mountains to Granada.

### Frigiliana

A visit to the nearby sleepy hilltop village of Frigiliana, with its cobbled alleyways and pristine white houses, splashed with geraniums and bougainvillea is a must. Frigiliana has been awarded the title of 'Prettiest village in Andalucía' and is famous for its pottery and sweet wine.

### Maro

This pretty village, 4 km (2 miles) east of Nerja, enjoys lovely views from its church square over a sandy cove. Look out for the aqueduct on the other side of the main road near the turn-off to the village.

### Salobreña

A spectacular Moorish castle dominates this attractive town surrounded by sugar-cane plantations. At the foot of the hill is a 16th-century church.

## TAKING A BREAK

**El Gato Negro £** A few doors on from Los Barriles, this charmingly ramshackle Italian restaurant serves up super-cheap pizza and pasta, accompanied by blaring Pavarotti. Take an outside table for some prime people watching. ⓐ Calle de Carabeo 19 ⓣ 952 52 56 11

**Kronox £** Perfect spot for people watching over breakfast or coffee. ⓐ Plaza Balcón de Europa, 7

**Restaurante Pacomari £** This deceptively large restaurant is ideal for families on a budget. Choose from the exceptionally good value set menu, kids' menu or the full works with traditional Spanish paella, fish dishes and barbecued meats. ⓐ Calle Gloria 4 ⓣ 952 52 01 38.

**Los Barriles ££** Buzzing little tapas bar specializing in chargrilled *chorizo* (spicy Spanish sausage) and other meats, enjoyed at upturned barrels. ⓐ Calle de Carabeo 5

## AFTER DARK

### Restaurants
**Del Toscano £** Authentic pizzas served in a cosy restaurant just off Calle Cristo. ⓐ Calle Gloria ⓣ 952 52 30 88 ⓒ Closed Wed

**Haveli £** A popular Indian Tandoori restaurant with garden terrace. ⓐ Calle Cristo 42 ⓣ 952 52 42 97 ⓒ Open until late

**Marisquería La Marina £** The freshest seafood tapas in town. ⓐ Plaza la Marina ⓣ 952 52 12 99

**Antonio ££** Waterfront restaurant serving fish and tapas. ⓐ Paseo Marítimo 12, Almuñecar ⓣ 958 63 00 20

**La Bodega ££** Authentic wine bar stacked with barrels. ⓐ Plaza La Marina
ⓣ 952 52 52 04 ⓛ 20.00–23.00 Thur–Tues

**Casa Maro ££** Delightful restaurant in a beautifully restored eccentric
old house in a lovely quiet spot near the church. ⓐ Calle Maro
ⓣ 952 52 52 04

**Chiringuito El Peñón ££** Super location on a rocky promontory just above
the waves. Fish and meat barbecue every evening in summer.
ⓐ Playa del Peñón, Salobreña ⓣ 958 61 05 38

**La Sardina Alegre ££** Old-fashioned little seafood restaurant specializing
in Basque cuisine. ⓐ Calle Almirante Fernandiz/Calle Cristo 5 ⓣ 952 52 13
87 ⓛ Closed Tue, and mid-Nov–mid-Dec

**Verano Azul ££** A smart, lively place serving good Spanish dishes – lots of
tables outside. ⓐ Calle Almirante Ferrandiz 31

**Casa Luque £££** Elegant dining in lovely gardens overlooking the sea.
ⓐ Plaza Canavas 2 ⓣ 952 52 10 04

**The Garden Restaurant £££** A well-established place in a wonderful
setting. ⓐ Frigiliana ⓣ 952 53 31 85

### Nightlife
**El Burro Blanco £** Live flamenco and international music. ⓐ Calle Gloria 3
ⓣ 952 52 42 00

**Maui ££** Brightly painted Scandinavian and English bar with a line in
vodka jellies. ⓐ Plaza Tutti Frutti

**Pub Rio ££** Dance under the stars in this tropical-style open-air disco.
ⓐ Rambla del Rio Chillar. ⓛ 24.00–07.00 July–Sept

# Almerimar

The Costa de Almería begins east of Motril, and the scenery takes on a ghostly pallor. Pale, desiccated hills loom inland, while vast expanses of plastic horticultural sheeting stretch over the coastal plains, sheltering prodigious quantities of intensively grown fruit and salad vegetables – strawberries, peppers, cucumbers, melons. The sheer scale of the enterprise is awesome. This is one section of the coast where agricultural land is still more valuable than building plots. Much of the produce grown in the makeshift hothouses around El Ejido ends up in British supermarket trolleys.

But there's more to the Costa de Almería than market gardening. The fast highway that slices arrow-straight across the Campo de Dalías bypasses an apron of coastal plain containing several fast-growing resorts. None of these places has anything like the high profile of, say, Torremolinos or Marbella. But visitors to these little-known areas may be pleasantly surprised by the long expanses of unspoilt beach on their doorsteps. The region also lays claim to an unexpectedly wild and watery world of reedbeds and saltmarsh lagoons, haunt of migrant flamingos and huge dragonflies. Amid these contrasting landscapes, the gleaming designer-built marina resort of Almerimar erupts like a strange space-station oasis. Fringed by an immaculate golf course as well as an approach-drive aglow with pink oleander, its state-of-the-art quaysides bristle with shops, restaurants and bars. Glass-bottomed boat trips and sub-aqua activities make the most of the clear, warm water.

## TAKING A BREAK

### Restaurants
**Heladería Cafetería Noray £** Ice creams and fruit juices, along with other drinks. Spacious waterfront terrace. ➌ Dársena 3, Puerto Deportivo ❶ 950 49 75 53 ❶ Until 23.30 Sat–Thur

● *The pristine marina at Almerimar*

**Cafeteria Milenio ££** Popular café on the waterfront, serving coffee and cakes until late. ⓐ Puerto Deportivo

**El Segoviano ££** Traditional Castilian cooking, including suckling pig. ⓐ Dársena 2 , Puerto Deportivo ⓣ 950 49 75 44 ⓛ 20.00–23.00 Mon–Sat

**El Náutico £££** One of the prettiest of Almerimar's waterfront buildings, in Moorish Andalucían style with terrace tables outside. Specialities include clams, carpaccio, partridge in vinegar. ⓐ Dársena 1, Puerto Deportivo ⓣ 950 49 71 62 ⓛ 19.30–23.30

**Nightlife**
**Edificio Jaleo** Literally meaning 'stir it up', this complex houses a number of clubs and is a good bet for a night on the dance floor. ⓐ Dársena 1, Paseo Poniente ⓛ Until late

# Roquetas

Roquetas is a surprisingly populous area, a former fishing port recently expanded by the burgeoning horti-business of intensive cultivation under plastic that occupies many acres of the local hinterland. Many of the workers who service this greenhouse empire live in Roquetas town. The newer resort of Roquetas de Mar lies some way southwest of the town (follow signs to 'Urbanizaciones' or 'Roquetas Costa').

Architecturally, Roquetas is an unusual place. Avoiding the stark high-rises that have fallen out of favour on many parts of the Mediterranean coast, Roquetas has opted for a brand of Andalucían post-modernism – all fantasy turrets and uneven rooflines. Certainly it is more attractive and interesting to look at than many modern resorts. Accommodation has an upmarket air, and there's a mix of nationalities, including German and Belgian visitors. The long seafront encompasses several town beaches, but the main resort strand is **Playa Serena**, a Blue Flag beach.

## THINGS TO SEE & DO

### Mariopark

A jolly water park promising family fun with black holes, kamikaze slides and toboggans. ⓐ Camino Las Salinas ⓣ 950 32 75 75 ⓦ www.mariopark.com ⓛ 11.00–19.00, closed winter ⓘ Admission charge

### Punta Entinas–Sabinar

The peaceful saltmarsh habitats between Roquetas de Mar's Playa Serena and Almerimar are now a protected nature reserve and a paradise for wildlife and birdwatchers. Over 200 species of birds can be found in a 16 km (10 mile) coastal strip of lagoons and reedbeds, including flamingos at certain times of year. Unusual plants, insects, lizards and toads also live in the marshes.

### Sail & Surf Roquetas

Windsurfing and sailing fans are well catered for, with equipment hire and tuition in front of Hotel Bahía Serena on Playa Serena.

ⓐ In front of Hotel Bahía Serena ① 659 04 77 92 Ⓦ www.surfroquetas.com

## TAKING A BREAK

**Cafetería Balix £** Spanning the cultural divides, this agreeable little place obliges with German, English or Spanish-style breakfasts and much else besides. Central and friendly. ⓐ Urb. Playa Serena ① 950 33 49 32

**Heladería Alicante £** Mouth-watering range of ice creams and cakes to eat in or take away. ⓐ Avenida del Mediterráneo

**Restaurante Chino Shanghai £** Good value lunch menu and over 100 oriental favourites. ⓐ Avenida del Mediterráneo

**Suzi's ££** Tapas bar serving a range of seafood snacks (smoked sardines, small clams, etc). ⓐ Avenida Playa Serena

## AFTER DARK

### Restaurants
**Christine and Dick's £** English-run bar and restaurant serving home-cooked English food and full Sunday roasts. Live music at weekends.
ⓐ Edificio Albatross ◑ Open Mon–Sat 18.00–late, and Sun 12.00–late.

**Al Baida ££** Sample typical Almerian shellfish dishes at this excellent fish restaurant, or move straight on to the wine in the **Bodega Al Baida** next door. ⓐ Avenida de las Gaviotas 94 ① 950 33 38 21 ◑ Closed Mon

**La Alpujarra ££** A good bet with dishes to suit everyone, including tasty anglerfish with cider and broad beans. ⓐ Urb. Playa Serena
① 950 33 38 59 ◑ 13.00–16.00, 19.00–24.00, closed Tues

# Aguadulce

The oldest of the three Costa de Almería resorts, the quieter Aguadulce has more traditional-looking hotels interspersed with greenery along its pleasant palm-lined seafront. Mostly a family resort, the port area livens up in the evenings. The long beach is less busy than further down the coast, and is meticulously combed by machines in the early mornings.

## THINGS TO DO

La Puebla del Vicar, just off the N340 a few kilometres west of Aguadulce, holds a colourful Sunday morning market selling anything and everything: local ceramics, leatherware, fruit and nuts. Don't confuse this place with the pretty village called Vicar, further inland.

## TAKING A BREAK

**Café Almanecer ££** All-day watering hole that serves tapas the old-fashioned way, free with every drink you order. Glass fronted, comfy wicker armchairs and an outdoor terrace make the most of the sea view all year round. ⓐ Puerto Deportivo ⓣ 950 55 28 65 ⓛ 07.00–03.00

**Cerveceria el Malagueño ££** A casual little restaurant with friendly staff and unexpectedly good fish and meat tapas. Or just enjoy a cold drink and the marina view. ⓐ Puerto Deportivo ⓣ 950 34 64 52 ⓛ Mon–Sun

**La Gruta ££** This excellent restaurant in a cave near the sea, specialises in grilled meats, and has a good wine list. Try the venison with truffles. ⓐ Some distance out of town above the Almería road, Carretera N340, Km 436 ⓣ 950 23 93 35 ⓛ Evenings only, closed Sun and the first two weeks of Oct and Feb

---

● *Gardens at the Alhambra, Granada*

# Sevilla

Sevilla (Seville) is the capital of Andalucía, Spain's fourth city, and one of its most exciting. Majestic, lively and passionately Spanish, it is the home of *Carmen*, *Don Juan* and the cradle of flamenco. As a local saying goes: 'He who hasn't seen Sevilla, has seen no wondrous thing.'

Sevilla is easy to explore on foot, with most of the main sights clustered alongside or near the Guadalquivir river. Be sure to visit the picturesque Santa Cruz district east of the cathedral, with its narrow streets of whitewashed buildings, shaded squares and flower-filled patios, and Triana, across the river, especially popular at night with its countless tapas bars and tiny restaurants. It is here that flamenco is said to have been created and, for many, Triana is still *the* place in Spain to experience spontaneous flamenco and *sevillanas* dancing.

## THINGS TO SEE & DO

### Antigua Fábrica de Tabacos (Old Tobacco Factory)

The 18th-century tobacco factory is where the beautiful gypsy Carmen from Bizet's opera worked as a cigar maker, before being stabbed to death by her lover. It is now part of the university and is not open to the public, but the exterior is stunning.

ⓐ Calle San Fernando

### Casa de Pilatos (Pilate's House)

Pilate's House is one of Sevilla's finest palaces, dating from the early 1500s and copied from Pontius Pilate's Jerusalem abode by the visiting Marquis of Tarifa. A Renaissance facade conceals typical Moorish courtyard gardens containing classical statues and lovely Mudéjar ceilings.

ⓐ Plaza de Pilatos 1 ⓣ 954 22 52 98 ⓛ Ground floor 09.00–19.00 (summer); 09.00–18.00 (winter). First floor 10.00–14.00, 15.00–19.00 (summer); 10.00–14.00, 15.00–18.00 (winter) ⓘ Admission charge

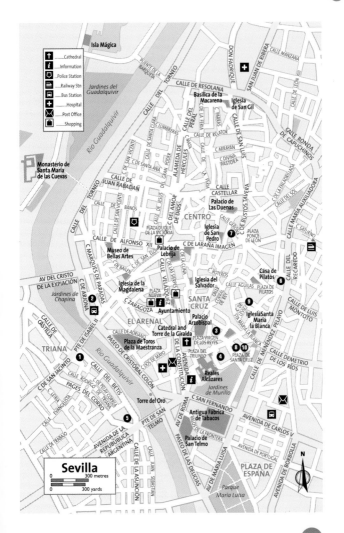

Cathedral
Information
Police Station
Railway Stn
Bus Station
Hospital
Post Office
Shopping

Isla Mágica

Jardines del Guadalquivir

Monastério de Santa María de las Cuevas

Basílica de la Macarena
Iglesia de San Gil

CALLE DE RESOLANA

Rio Guadalquivir

CALLE DE JUAN RABADÁN

CENTRO

Palacio de Las Dueñas

Iglesia de San Pedro **7**

Museo de Bellas Artes

Palacio de Lebrija

Casa de Pilatos **6**

Iglesia de la Magdalena

Iglesia del Salvador

Iglesia Santa María la Blanca **9**

Ayuntamiento

SANTA CRUZ

EL ARENAL

Palacio Arzobispal

TRIANA **1**

Catedral and Torre de la Giralda

Plaza de Toros de la Maestranza

**3**

**8** **10**

Reales Alcázares

Torre del Oro

Jardines de Murilla

**5**

Antigua Fábrica de Tabacos

Palacio de San Telmo

PLAZA DE ESPAÑA

Parque María Luisa

**Sevilla**

0 ___ 300 metres
0 ___ 300 yards

N

**GETTING ABOUT**

Open-top bus tours are a great way to see the city. Buses leave half-hourly from the Torre del Oro by the river, and cover all the main sites. **Sevirama bus tours** ⓐ Torre del Oro ❶ 954 56 06 93

A romantic way to see the sights, hour-long river cruises run daily every 30 minutes from 11.00 to 22.00 from the quayside below the Torre del Oro. Also a night-time cruise (*crucero de noche*) with an on-board fiesta. **Cruceros Turísticos** ⓐ Torre del Oro ❶ 954 21 13 96

### Catedral and Torre de la Giralda (Giralda Tower)

This unmissable building is the largest Gothic cathedral in the world and houses a staggering 43 chapels as well as Christopher Colombus' (alleged) tomb. It was originally constructed on the site of a mosque whose only remaining feature is the 70m- (230 ft)-high minaret. The views from the top are worth the climb.

ⓐ Plaza Virgen de los Reyes ❶ 957 56 33 21 ❷ 11.00–17.00 Mon–Fri, 11.00–16.00 Sat, 14.00–16.00 Sun

### Isla Mágica

This fantasy theme park on the Expo 92 exhibition site takes you back four centuries to the discovery of the New World, with spectacular multi-media presentations based on the adventures of the explorers.

ⓐ Pabellón de España, Isla de la Cartuja ❶ 902 16 17 16
ⓦ www.Islamagica.es ❷ Opening times vary; generally 11.00–23.00 (summer) ❶ Admission charge

### Museo de Bellas Artes (Fine Arts Museum)

In a former convent, this houses an important collection of Sevillian baroque masterpieces, including works by Murillo, Zurbarán and Juan de Mesa, and is one of the country's major galleries.

ⓐ Plaza del Museo 9 ❶ 954 22 07 90 ❷ 15.00–20.00 Tues, 09.00–20.00 Wed–Sat, 09.00–14.00 Sun ❶ Admission free with EU passport

### Parque María Luisa
Beautifully laid out gardens close to the Plaza de España. Wander around on foot or in a horse and carriage.

### Plaza de España
Constructed for a major exhibition in 1929, this monumental semicircular plaza on the east side of the city is one of Sevilla's most striking public spaces, featuring grandly towered buildings, fountain pools and bright, ceramic tiles representing all of Spain's 51 provinces.

### Reales Alcázares (Royal Fortress)
This magnificent 14th-century Arab fortress is one of the best surviving examples of Moorish architecture in Europe and not to be missed. It also has beautiful gardens.
ⓐ Plaza del Triunfo, Puerta del Leon ☎ 954 22 71 63 🕐 10.30–17.00 Tues–Sat, 10.30–13.00 Sun, closed Mon ❶ Admission charge

### Torre del Oro (Golden Tower)
The Moorish 'Golden Tower', built in 1220 to guard the Guadalquivir river, was originally covered in golden tiles and linked to a second 'Silver Tower' by a large chain. Today this impressive 12-sided building houses a small maritime museum.
ⓐ Paseo de Cristóbal Colón ☎ 954 22 24 19 🕐 10.00–14.00 Tues–Fri, 11.00–14.00 Sat and Sun, closed Aug ❶ Admission charge (free Tues)

## AFTER DARK

### Restaurants

**Kiosko de las Flores £ ❶** A splendid old-fashioned little *freiduría* (fried fish shop) near the Puente Isabel II, specializing in fried fish and clams. ⓐ Calle Betis ❶ 954 27 45 76 Ⓦ www.kioskdelasflores.com

**La Mandragora £ ❷** One of very few vegetarian restaurants in town. ⓐ Calle Albuera 11 ❶ 954 22 01 84 ⓛ 14.00–16.00 Tues–Sat, 21.30–23.30 Thur–Sat, closed Sun, Mon and Aug

**Cervecería Giralda ££ ❸** Atmospheric tapas bar in a converted Arab bath house, just a stone's throw from the cathedral. ⓐ Calle Mateos Gago 1 ❶ 954 22 74 35 ⓛ Open daily

**Hostería del Laurel ££ ❹** A lovely old inn with a tiled tapas bar, in the heart of Santa Cruz. ⓐ Plaza de los Venerables 5 ❶ 954 22 02 95 Ⓦ www.hosteriadellaurel.com ⓛ Open daily

**Ox's ££ ❺** A highly regarded *asador* (grill-room) on the Triana riverbank. Basque fish specialities and steaks. ⓐ Calle Betis 61 ❶ 954 27 95 85 ⓛ 12.00–17.00, 20.00–24.00 Tues–Sat

**Restaurante Becerríta ££ ❻** Sophisticated restaurant and tapas bar next to the Murillo gardens, serving tasty modern versions of traditional Andalucían dishes. Try the cuttlefish in ink, pork in crab sauce, or ox-tail croquettes. ⓐ Calle Recaredo 9 ❶ 954 41 20 57 ⓛ Closed Sun eve and Aug

**El Rinconcillo ££ ❼** Dating back to the 17th century and one of the best tapas bars in town. ⓐ Calle Gerona 42 ❶ 954 22 31 83 ⓛ 13.00–16.30, 19.30–24.00, closed last two weeks of July

🔺 *Plaza de España, Sevilla*

**La Albahaca £££** ❽ Set in a typical Andalucían house with terrace, this elegant restaurant is a favourite with Sevillanos. ⓐ Plaza de Santa Cruz 12 ☎ 954 22 07 14 🕐 13.00–16.00, 20.00–24.00 Mon–Sat

### Nightlife

Besides its famous tapas bars and *terrazas de verano* (open-air music bars set up temporarily along the waterfront in summer), Sevilla has many other nightspots. Calle Betis (Triana waterfront) livens up as the evening progresses, while the cafés and bars near Santa María la Blanca make an ideal spot for watching the world go by. Some of the flamenco shows on offer in Sevilla are very touristy. Try local bars for these typical *sevillanas* evenings instead.

**La Carbonería ££** ❾ Renowned music bar for flamenco, blues and rock, tucked away in back streets in former coal merchant's premises. Livens up late; best on Monday and Thursday. ⓐ Calle Levíes 18 ☎ 954 21 44 60

**Los Gallos £££** ❿ One of the top flamenco shows in town. ⓐ Plaza de Santa Cruz ☎ 954 21 69 81 🌐 www.tablaolosgallos.com 🕐 Performances at 20.00 and 23.30 ❶ Admission charge

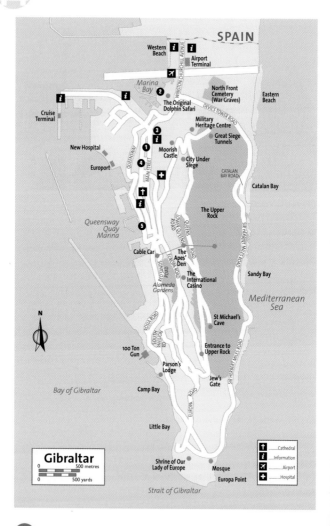

Gibraltar

# Gibraltar (UK)

Gibraltar is a towering chunk of ancient limestone, known as 'The Rock', which guards the narrow entrance to the Mediterranean. Gibraltar Town is very like a British town, but with a suntan. The streets, phone boxes, cars, currency, pubs and shops are all British – but the climate and the beaches are definitely Mediterranean. Gibraltar's VAT-free status makes it a popular place for a shopping spree.

You need to show your passport on entering and leaving Gibraltar. Border formalities are less protracted than they used to be, but motorists may be better off parking in La Línea, on the Spanish side, if queues look slow. On Sunday, many shops and sights are closed and the cable car doesn't operate.

## THINGS TO SEE & DO

A quick visit to Gibraltar's museum provides an invaluable historic insight before taking the cable car up to the top of the Rock to admire its many sights and the stupendous views. A blanket 'Nature Reserve' charge is made to enter any of the sights at the 'Top of the Rock'. On a guided tour, you can get an all-in deal. Sights are generally open 10.00–19.00 (summer), 10.00–17.30 (winter).

### The Apes' Den
Halfway up the Rock are the famous Barbary apes – the only group of wild primates remaining in Europe. It is said that as long as they are here, Gibraltar will remain British. Hang on carefully to your belongings and don't feed them, even if your taxi driver encourages you to.

### Dolphin watching
Trips to observe three species of dolphin that swim in the bay are available year-round. The Original Dolphin Safari uses a glass-bottomed boat.
ⓐ Marina Bay complex ⓣ 00350 71914 ⓦ www.dolphinsafari.gi

### Europa Point

On a clear day, you can see Africa from the southernmost point of the Rock – the 'Tip of Europe'. ① No admission charge

### Great Siege Tunnels

This vast network (48 km/29 miles) of tunnels resembling a Swiss cheese were dug into the rock in 1782 so that the British forces could better position their cannons at a great height, thus enabling them to win the Great Siege.

### Moorish Castle

Only one tower remains of this ancient 8th-century Moorish Castle, where once the people of Gibraltar sheltered and took refuge from marauding pirates who virtually destroyed the town.

### St Michael's Cave

St Michael's Cave is the largest of the group of caves on Gibraltar. Once home to groups of Neolithic people, its dramatic rock formations now provide the backdrop for concerts and fashion shows. Legend has it that there is an underground tunnel in one of the caves that leads under the Straits to Africa.

## TAKING A BREAK

### Restaurants & bars

**The Star Bar £** ❶  Reputedly the oldest pub on the Rock, this friendly little bar is as good a place as any to sample a traditional English 'fry up' or fish and chips in the sun. ⓐ Parliament Lane ☎ 00350 75924

**Bianca's ££** ❷  Relaxed restaurant overlooking the marina, good for nachos and sangria in the sun or a full-blown dinner. All the usual pizzas, meat and fish dishes, as well as a few surprises like banana pizza and steak stuffed with prawns. ⓐ 6/7 Admiral's Walk ☎ 00350 73379 🕐 09.00–late

▲ *View of 'The Rock'*

**Café Solo ££** ❸  Popular restaurant on the piazza, serving modern European dishes with an Italian bias. Excellent duck as well as salads, pastas and pizzas. ⓐ Grand Casemates Square ❶ 00350 44449 ● Daily for breakfast and dinner

**The Clipper ££** ❹  Hearty pub grub and Sunday roasts in a lively atmosphere. International sports events shown on big screen TVs. ⓐ 78b Irish Town ❶ 00350 79791 ● 09.30–24.00

**Claus on the Rock £££** ❺  One of Gibraltar's smartest restaurants, overlooking some dazzling boats berthed in its smartest marina. Expect inventive international cuisine of a high standard, together with a good wine list and cocktails. ⓐ Queensway Quay ❶ 00350 48686

# Ronda

The old town of Ronda is one of Andalucía's most spectacular and historic towns, famous for its breath-taking scenery, its fine Arab baths and palaces and the oldest bullring in Spain. You will only appreciate its full drama as you enter the town, split in half by a gaping river gorge, El Tajo. The remarkable gorge is spanned by an impressive arched bridge, while tall, whitewashed houses lean from its precipitous brink.

Local legend tells that God, fed-up with the constant squabbling of the people of Ronda, sent a huge bolt of lightning down to earth and split the city in two, with the women in one half and the men in the other. This arrangement was so unpopular that they built the bridge across the gorge to reunite the community.

Today, south of the gorge, **La Ciudad** (the old Moorish town) retains its Moorish plan, with many of its fine mansions and the now-Catholic church of Santa María la Mayor, once the town's main mosque. To the north lies El Mercadillo, the new town.

Ronda is the most famous of Andalucía's romantic *pueblos blancos*, the so-called 'white towns' built by the Moors in the 13th century to fend off the harsh rays of the sun. Its stunning location has frequently been used in Hollywood films, including *Carmen* and *For Whom the Bell Tolls*.

There are some excellent walks around Ronda. One without too much climbing is the footpath called Paseo Blas Infante, which begins behind the *parador* (state-owned hotel housed in an historic building) and leads along the brink of the gorge. An evening stroll along here gives wonderful views. Take your camera.

## THINGS TO SEE & DO

### Baño Arabes (Moorish baths)

This 13th-century bath house is the best preserved example in Europe, and still functions today.

ⓐ The Riverside ⓣ 952 87 38 89 ⓛ 10.00–13.30 Tues, 09.30–15.00 Wed–Sat, 10.00–14.00 Sun, closed Mon ⓘ Admission charge

● *Ronda and the impressive El Tajo gorge*

### La Casa del Rey Moro (Mansion of the Moorish Kings)

This 18th-century mansion overlooking the gorge was built on much older Moorish foundations. Although not open to the public, the house has an ancient underground stairway, which leads right down to the

river through terraced gardens. Cut out of the rock by Christian slaves, these 365 steps guaranteed a water supply to the people of the town, even in times of siege.

ⓐ Cuesta de Santo Domingo 17 ⓣ 952 18 72 00 ⓛ Gardens and stairway 10.00–20.00 (summer); 10.00–19.00 (winter) ❶ Admission charge

## Plaza de Toros (Bullring)

The bullring, built in 1785, is one of the oldest and most beautiful in Spain. It was here that Pedro Romero, the founder of modern bullfighting, evolved today's style of fighting bulls on foot rather than on horseback. Nowadays, the bullring is only used for special fiestas, but the museum is well worth a visit.

ⓐ Calle Virgen de la Paz 15 ⓣ 952 87 41 32 ⓛ 10.00–20.00 ❶ Admission charge

## El Tajo Gorge

Three bridges span the gorge: the Moorish Puente de San Miguel looks over the ancient Arab baths; the Puente Viejo (Old Bridge) was built in 1616 and the not-so-new Puente Nuevo (New Bridge), built in the late 18th century, boasts unforgettable views and is the symbol of Ronda. The gorge, at its highest point, drops over 90 m (300 ft) to the Guadalevin river below, and has a rather bloody past. The architect of the Puente Nuevo fell to his death here while attempting to catch his hat. In the 18th century, injured horses from the bullring were flung over the cliffs. During the Spanish Civil War, over 500 Nationalist prisoners were thrown into the gorge by Republicans.

## TAKING A BREAK

**Café Alba £** A popular breakfast spot, serving delicious coffee, piping hot chocolate and *churros* (akin to a doughnut). ⓐ Calle Espinel 44 ⓣ 952 19 09 53

**El Corralillo £** This clean, brightly tiled café in a covered passage is a good place to rest your feet midway through a shopping spree. Good *churros*, breakfasts and snacks. ⓐ Calle Espinel 40 ⓣ 952 87 77 33

**Jerez £** Straightforward, authentic local dishes like *migas* Ronda-style (deep-fried breadcrumbs) in a quiet corner behind the bullring. Shady terrace tables in summer. **ⓐ** Paseo Blas Infante 2 **ⓣ** 952 87 20 98 **ⓦ** www.restaurantejerez.com

**Doña Pepa ££** Well respected, family-run restaurant offering traditional local dishes like rabbit, partridge and quail in garlic. Their separate café-bar opposite serves *bocadillos* (sandwiches) and freshly squeezed orange juice. **ⓐ** Plaza del Socorro 10 **ⓣ** 952 87 47 77

## AFTER DARK

### Restaurants & bars
**Bar Las Castañuelas £** A lively local bar where you can enjoy a glass of *fino* (sherry) accompanied by inexpensive, traditional tapas. **ⓐ** Calle Jerez 3 **ⓣ** 952 87 61 78

**Pedro Romero ££** Regional specialities served opposite the famous bullring, in a restaurant decorated with fascinating bull-fighting memorabilia. Try the local favourite, *rabo de toro* (oxtail). **ⓐ** Virgen de la Paz 18 **ⓣ** 952 87 11 10 **ⓦ** www.ronda.net/pedroromero

**Peña Flamenco Tobalo ££** Some claim that Ronda (and not Sevilla) is the birthplace of flamenco. Live shows take place in Bar la Plazuela most Fridays. Telephone to check. **ⓐ** Calle Artesanos **ⓣ** 952 87 41 77 **ⓘ** Admission charge

**Parador de Ronda £££** The most perfectly situated hotel in town, overlooking the ravine just next to the Puente Nuevo. The food is also delicious: expect traditional Andalucían favourites like *ajo blanco* (cold garlic soup), roast kid and rabbit. For pudding, try the local speciality *yemas rondenas* (sweet egg yolks). **ⓐ** Plaza Espana **ⓣ** 952 87 72 00

# White towns

Andalucía is full of huddled towns and villages that dazzle on the hilltops. Each consists of a typical Moorish tangle of narrow alleyways lined by whitewashed cottages and flower-filled patios, and many are crowned with castles. Some lie quite close to the coast, and are mentioned elsewhere in this guide (Mijas in the hills behind Fuengirola, Frigiliana near Nerja, or Mojácar on the Costa de Almería).

Many of the best-known *pueblos blancos* (white towns) lie near Ronda. Organised excursions visit a few of them from the coastal resorts, but if you have your own transport you can choose your own picnic route

⬥ Casares, *pueblo blanco*

through some splendid rugged scenery (it is unlikely you would be able to cover all the villages in one day). On the journey from the coast into the rugged Serranía de Ronda mountains, watch out for mountain hare, deer, wild partridge and the endangered Spanish ibex (wild goat), while golden eagles, lesser kestrels and griffon vultures wheel in the sky. Pick up a tourist office leaflet for some itinerary ideas, but here are some suggestions.

- **Arcos de la Frontera** Reaching this sizeable town involves a hair-raising climb through the old quarter. A *parador* and a fine Gothic church teeter on the edge of a spectacular cliff where hawks practise hang-gliding.
- **Benaoján** Famed for its caves. The Cueva de la Pileta contains prehistoric wall-paintings.
- **Casares** White houses spill down a steep hillside.
- **Gaucín** The ridge-top setting with marvellous views attracts many visitors – some set up home here.
- **Grazalema** One of the prettiest of all the *pueblos*. The tourist office probably won't tell you that it has the highest rainfall in Spain (hence its surprisingly lush surroundings).
- **Jimena de la Frontera** A ruined Moorish castle dominates a landscape of cork oaks, olives and fighting bulls.
- **Medina Sidonia** An aristocratic town of imposing palaces.
- **Olvera** A dramatic landslide of glittering houses below a castle.
- **Setenil** A river-gorge of volcanic tufa adds an unusual setting to Setenil's white houses; some have roofs of natural rock.
- **Ubrique** A thriving leather industry keeps souvenir-hunters happy in this bustling town.
- **Vejer de la Frontera** It's a long drive to this little place near Cape Trafalgar, but Vejer is one of the most memorable and traditional of these African-looking settlements.
- **Zahara de la Sierra** Now declared a national monument, this striking village of red-tiled houses on an arid castle-crowned rock will keep your camera snapping.

# Mijas

Just 8 km (5 miles) inland from the modern urban sprawl of Fuengirola, set among tranquil pine groves on the edge of the Sierra de Mijas mountains, this picture-postcard *pueblo blanco* is a photographer's dream. This is Andalucía at its picturesque best, with hilly, cobbled streets, wrought-iron balconies cascading with flowers, donkey taxis, unique square bullring and breathtaking coastal views.

Like most of the villages situated in this region, Mijas (which is pronounced '*me*-hass') has Roman, Phoenician and Moorish origins. Its present layout dates back to Moorish times, when the village served as a granary for Fuengirola and a defence against the Christians. In the 17th and 18th centuries, Mijas housed the workers of the now-disused marble quarries in the hills. The marble cut from these quarries was used to build the cathedral in Málaga and the Alcazaba in Córdoba. It then became a farming community until the tourism boom of the 1960s and 1970s.

At first Mijas was a must-see for every visitor then, after a while, many of the foreign visitors decided it was a great place to live and began to build property on the gentle slopes of the Sierra, between Mijas and the coast. Today, expat residents outnumber Spaniards, and the views from the village towards the Mediterranean are dotted with their luxury villas, sparkling azure swimming pools and golf courses, rather than avocado-pear plantations.

The village is still very much a tourist attraction, thriving on its local handicrafts of ceramics, leather and lace. Its dazzling white streets are filled with bars and restaurants. Horse-drawn carriages or *burro taxis* (donkey taxis) carry visitors away from the crowded centre, up the steep, narrow parts, where Mijas has conserved its rustic charm and sleepy Andalucían atmosphere.

Wander the quaint backstreets of Mijas to avoid the crowds

## THINGS TO SEE & DO

### Carromato de Max (Museum of Miniatures)

This must be the most peculiar museum on the entire coast, with such exhibits (all under magnifying glasses) as the 'seven wonders of the world' painted on a toothpick and a bullfight painted on a lentil.

ⓐ Avenida del Compás ⓣ 952 48 58 20 ⓛ 10.00–22.00 ⓘ Admission charge

### Ermita del Calvario (Chapel of Calvary)

For the best views in town, climb up to the tiny chapel of the Calvary, high above the village. The walk, through cool pine groves, following a trail of black iron crosses, takes about 30 minutes. At the top, you will be well rewarded with breathtaking views to Gibraltar and Africa.

### Golf

Mijas is famous for its top-quality golf courses, drawing thousands of enthusiasts every year. Los Lagos and Los Olivos are popular courses near Mijas, as is **Mijas-Golf**

ⓐ Camino viejo de Coín, Km 3.5 ⓣ 952 47 68 43 ⓦ www.mijasgolf.org
ⓛ Open daily

### Tennis

Mijas's tennis club, founded by the late Lew Hoad, has courts to rent, special coaching programmes and mini tournaments. Other facilities include a swimming pool and beauty centre. **Campo de Tenis Lew Hoad**

ⓐ Carretera de Mijas, Km 3.5 ⓣ 952 47 48 58 ⓦ www.tennis-spain.com
ⓛ Open daily

## TAKING A BREAK

### Restaurants & bars

**Bar Porras £** This friendly, no-frills bar provides a good opportunity to meet the locals over a beer and a plate of tapas. ⓐ Plaza Libertad 3
ⓣ 952 48 50 41

## SHOPPING

**Amapola** Offers tiny pots, jewellery and other trinkets decorated with dried wild flowers from the countryside. ⓐ Alcazaba, Plaza de la Constitucíon ☎ 952 48 62 54

**Artesanía de España** Probably the best choice of pottery in town. ⓐ Calle Málaga 2 ☎ 952 48 62 03

**Artesanía Rocío** A tiny, old-fashioned shop selling Spanish lace. ⓐ Pasaje Salvador Cantón Jimenez ☎ 610 03 68 18 (mobile)

**La Casa del Arte de la Seda** Silk shawls and elaborate, hand-made jewellery. ⓐ Calle Málaga 20 ☎ 952 59 04 53

**Guantería Costa del Sol** Leather bags, belts, wallets … and how about an extra suitcase for all your presents and souvenirs? ⓐ Calle Los Caños 17 ☎ 952 48 59 46

**El Shop** Try here for timeless yet useful gift ideas such as candlesticks and picture frames, hand-cast in brass and aluminium. ⓐ Alcazaba, Plaza de la Constitucíon ☎ 952 59 03 07

**Tamisa** Lladró porcelain, Mallorcan pearls and beautiful traditionally styled jewellery of filigree silver, brass and copper – a speciality of Mijas. ⓐ Alcazaba, Plaza de la Constitucíon ☎ 952 48 51 41 ⓦ www.tamisashop.com

**La Alcazaba** ££ Beautiful Moorish-looking restaurant offering great seafood and wonderful views from a prime clifftop location. ⓐ Alcazaba, Plaza de la Constitucíon ☎ 952 59 02 53 ⓛ Closed Mon

**El Mirlo Blanco** ££ 'The White Blackbird' is a thoroughly Spanish, family-run restaurant near the bullring. Don't miss the spider crab, or the *leche frita* (thick custard cut into squares then fried). Delicious! ⓐ Plaza de la Constitucíon 2 ☎ 952 48 57 00 ⓐ Closed Tues

**Restaurante Tamisa** ££ Mouth-watering menu of lamb, steak and other meats cooked on an outside barbecue, as well as more typical Spanish dishes. ⓐ Avenida Méjico 21 ☎ 952 59 04 78 ⓛ Closed Mon

⬢ The cool interior of Córdoba's Great Mosque

# Córdoba

Situated in the fertile valley of the Guadalquivir river, the ancient city of Córdoba remains comparatively untouched by tourism and is one of Andalucía's most precious jewels, a city of churches, mansions, museums and La Mezquita – a masterpiece of Islamic art and one of the largest mosques in the world.

## THINGS TO SEE & DO

### Judería (Jewish Quarter)

This is the prettiest district of Córdoba – a charming tangle of narrow, whitewashed streets and alleys, with brilliantly coloured flowers spilling over from every balcony. Wooden doors open onto some of the loveliest patios in Andalucía, adorned with fountains and blue ceramic tiles and shaded by palm and orange trees. One of the most picturesque streets is Calleja de las Flores. By day, you can also find some delightful souvenirs in its many small shops, and by night people flock to its restaurants and bars to sing flamenco and dance *sevillanas* (typical Sevillana dance).

### La Mezquita (The Great Mosque)

This is the most important Islamic monument in the western world, and no guidebook can adequately prepare you for its grandeur; you enter through a patio of orange trees into the ancient, dimly lit mosque – a forest of stone columns and double red and cream arches. For the most spectacular view of the city and the mountains beyond, climb what seems like thousands of steps to the top of La Mezquita's minaret tower. Your efforts will be well rewarded!

ⓐ Calle Cardenal Herrero 1 ❶ 957 47 05 12 ⏰ 10.00–18.00 Mon–Sat, 15.30–17.30 Sun. Last entry 30 mins before closing. Evening opening varies each month. Excellent access for visitors with disabilities
❶ Admission charge

### Palacio de Viana (Viana Palace)

This lovely 16th-century palace is the former seat of the Marquises of Viana. Its best feature is its 'Museum of Courtyards' – a dozen flower-filled patios, each one differently designed. They reach their peak of perfection in May, in time for the Fiesta de los Patios.

ⓐ Plaza Don Gome 2 ❶ 957 49 67 41 🕐 09.00–14.00 Mon–Sat (summer); 10.00–13.00, 16.00–18.00 Mon–Fri, 10.00–13.00 Sat (winter), closed 1–15 June ❶ Admission charge

### Plaza del Potro

Don't miss this atmospheric, old, cobbled square, named after the lively *potro* (colt) rearing above its fountain. Posada del Potro, a quaint old inn where Cervantes stayed, now houses the Casa de Cultura. Also here is the **Museo de Bellas Artes (Fine Arts Museum)**, containing orthodox works by a number of Spanish masters. ❶ 957 47 33 45 🕐 14.30–20.30 Tues, 09.00–20.30 Wed–Sat ❶ Admission free with EU passport.

## AFTER DARK

### Restaurants

**Il Pisto (aka Taberna San Miguel)** £ Come here for a wide choice of good-value tapas dishes. The spicy *chorizo* (Spanish sausage) and *patatas ailioli* (potatoes with garlic mayonnaise) are especially delicious.
ⓐ Plaza San Miguel 1 ❶ 957 47 01 66

**Rincon de Chico Medina** £ Unpretentious little tapas bar offering generous portions of Andalucían favourites at remarkably good prices.

> ### SHOPPING
> The main shops are along **Calle Conde de Gondomar** and **Calle Claudio Marcelo** on either side of **Plaza Tendillas**. There is also a clothes and crafts market every morning in **Plaza de la Corredera**.

⬥ *La Mezquita (see page 77)*

The *salmorejo* (local variation of *gazpacho*) is particularly good here.
ⓐ Calle Historiador Díaz del Moral 5 ☏ 957 48 28 08

**El Bandolero ££** Beautiful restaurant with attentive service and high quality tapas that have been officially voted the best in Córdoba. Try the Iberian pork or the exemplary *gazpacho*. A little pricey but worth it for the location, just outside La Mezquita. ⓐ Calle Torrijos 6–8 ☏ 957 47 64 91

**Casa Pepe de la Judería ££** One of Córdoba's best-loved restaurants. Try the *salmorejo* (salt of the Moors), a thicker variation of *gazpacho*, with ham and egg). ⓐ Calle A Romero 1 ☏ 957 20 07 44

**El Churrasco ££** This small, intimate restaurant is an old favourite in Córdoba. It specialises in grilled meats, served at tables on an attractive patio. ⓐ Calle A Romero 16 ☏ 957 29 08 19 ⓦ www.elchurrasco.com

**El Caballo Rojo £££** For a special occasion, this classic restaurant by La Mezquita is famous for its Andalucían dishes with an Arab influence.
ⓐ Calle Cardenal Herrero 28 ☏ 957 47 53 75 ⓦ www.elcaballorojo.com
❶ No wheelchair access

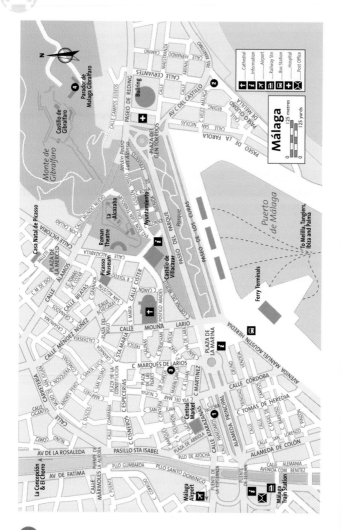

Málaga

# Málaga

Málaga is a bustling seaport, the sprawling capital of the Costa, the
second city of Andalucía and the sixth biggest city in Spain. You
either love it or you hate it, but there is no denying, it is one of the most
Spanish of cities – atmospheric and vibrant.

## THINGS TO SEE & DO

### La Alcazaba (Moorish Fortress)
The remains of an 11th-century Moorish fortress stand in attractive
fountain-splashed gardens high above the city. Its terraces afford
photogenic vistas of Málaga and its glittering bay.
ⓐ Calle Alcazabilla ☎ 952 22 00 43 🕐 09.30–13.30, 17.00–20.00 Tues–Fri,
10.00–14.00 Sat & Sun ❶ Admission charge

### Antequera
The town of Antequera is easily reached by car or public transport from
Málaga. It's usually a quiet town, but it livens up on Fridays when its
market is in full swing. Most of its monuments are shut on Mondays. The
old centre contains an impressive list of monuments, including several
large churches, a ruined Arab fortress (Alcazaba) and an archway (Arco
de los Gigantes) dating from the 16th century. Both the town hall
(Palacio Consistorial) and the museum (Museo Municipal) occupy fine
palaces. Antequera's most unusual sights, though, are its dolmen caves,
easily found on the approach road from Málaga. These megalithic
monuments are believed to be around 4,500 years old.

### Castillo de Gibralfaro (Gibralfaro Castle)
One of Málaga's great landmarks, this Moorish castle perched high above
the city was built sometime in the early 14th century on the site of an
ancient lighthouse. At the foot of the Castillo is a Roman amphitheatre.
ⓐ Monte de Gibralfaro ☎ 952 22 72 30 🕐 09.30–20.00
❶ Joint ticket with La Alcazaba

### Cathedral

Málaga's cathedral took more than 350 years to build. The original plans included two towers but the money ran out, so only one was completed, giving rise to the affectionate nickname, La Manquita ('the little one-armed woman').

ⓐ Calle Molina Lario ⓣ 952 21 59 17 ⓛ 10.00–12.45, 16.00–17.30 Mon–Sat, closed to sightseers on Sun ❶ Admission charge

### El Chorro

North of Málaga the River Guadalhorce cuts a dramatic gorge through sheer 30-m (100-ft) cliffs that make irresistible targets for rock-climbers. Above the gorge are the reservoir lakes, which supply most of Málaga's water. The scenery in this craggy area is spectacular, and offers many opportunities for walks and picnics.

### Jardin Botánico Histórico de la Concepción

An Englishwoman married to the Marquis of Casa Loring assembled this collection of rare and exotic plants, one of Spain's most important gardens.

ⓐ Carretera de las Pedrizas, Km 166 (off the Antequera road)
ⓣ 952 25 21 48 ⓛ 10.00–19.30 Tues–Sun ❶ Visits by guided tour only

### Picasso Museums

The artist Pablo Picasso was born in Málaga in 1881. His birthplace, the **Casa Natal de Picasso**, contains an exhibition of photographs of Picasso as a child, plus memorabilia and early works.

ⓐ Plaza de la Merced ⓣ 952 06 02 15 ⓛ 10.00–14.00, 17.00–20.00 Mon–Sat, 11.00–14.00 Sun ❶ Admission free

    In a nearby street, part of the former Museo de Bellas Artes, a 16th-century palace, has been restored to house the excellent **Picasso Museum**, containing around 140 major works. ⓐ Calle San Agustin 8
ⓣ 952 12 76 00 ⓦ www.museopicassomalaga.org ❶ Admission charge

## El Torcal

South of Antequera lies a weird wonderland of eroded limestone outcrops, which, in place, look like stacks of dinner plates. Rare plants and birds of prey colonize the region, which is one of Andalucía's most spectacular natural parks. The strange formations are best seen towards sundown, when the shadows are sharpest. There are regular excursions to El Torcal from the coastal resorts. For more information, contact the park information centre: **Centro de Visitantes.** ☎ 952 03 13 89 ⏰ 10.00–14.00, 15.00–17.00 (Nov–May); 10.00–14.00, 16.00–18.00 (June–Oct)

## TAKING A BREAK

Málaga is famed for its old *bodegas* (wine bars) and tapas bars, which provide a good opportunity to try local delicacies and the sweet local wine, while the smart seafront promenade boasts some of the best fish restaurants in the province.

**Antigua Casa del Guardia £ ❶** Atmospheric *bodega* founded in 1840, and lined with barrels. An excellent place to sample some of Málaga's sweet wines. ⓐ Calle Alameda Principal 18 ☎ 952 21 46 80

**Antonio Martín £££ ❷** A popular seafront restaurant specializing in seafood. ⓐ Paseo Marítimo ☎ 952 22 73 82

## AFTER DARK

### Restaurants
**Mesón lo Güeno ££ ❸** Elegant Spanish tapas restaurant. ⓐ Calle Marín Garcia 9 ☎ 952 22 30 48 ⏰ Daily for lunch and dinner

**Parador de Malaga Gibralfaro ££ ❹** This very special state-owned hotel and restaurant is set high on a wooded hill, and has breathtaking views along the coast. The food is very good, and the set menu is punctuated by tasty *amuses bouches*. ⓐ Castillo del Giralfaro ☎ 952 22 19 02

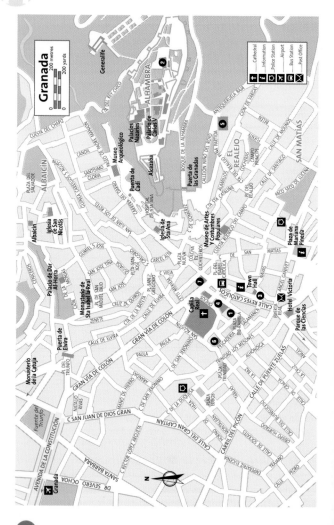

# Granada

If you only visit one city during your stay in Spain, it should be Granada, the historic city just two hours' drive from Málaga – set against a backdrop of snow-capped mountains of the Sierra Nevada – and home to the exquisite Alhambra Palace.

## THINGS TO SEE & DO

### Albaicín (Ancient Arab Quarter)

The Arab quarter's picturesque, cobbled streets of whitewashed houses cling to the hillside facing the Alhambra, punctuated by tiny fountain-filled squares and hidden patios of lemon trees, pomegranates and vines. Beyond the hill, a few of Granada's gypsy population still live in the Sacromonte cave dwellings. Some of the caves, such as Los Faroles, now stage flamenco spectacles, and the ones above Casa del Chapiz are popular weekend disco haunts during university term-time.

### Alhambra and Generalife

The Alhambra is one of the world's most remarkable, harmonious collections of 14th-century Arabic palaces, fortifications, domes and ornamental gardens, which represent the epitome of Moorish architecture with their mosaics, marble balustrades, carved wooden ceilings and fine filigree stonework. There are three distinct groups of buildings on Alhambra Hill: the Casa Real or Royal Palace – the real gem of the Alhambra, the Generalife gardens, and the oldest section, the Alcazaba, dating from the 10th to 13th centuries.
ⓐ Calle Real de la Alhambra ⓣ 958 22 09 12 ⓦ www.alhambra.org
ⓛ Daily from 08.30, with seasonal variations ⓘ Admission charge

### Capilla Real (Royal Chapel)

The impressive Royal Chapel, adjoining the vast Gothic cathedral, contains the tombs of the Catholic monarchs, Ferdinand and Isabella, who were the conquerors of Granada.

> ## VISITING THE SIGHTS
> A maximum of 8,800 visitors are allowed into the Alhambra each day, so you should reserve in advance via any branch of the BBV bank, including the one on Plaza Isabel la Católica (a small commission is charged; ask the tourist office for details). Timed combined tickets are issued for the Alhambra's various sections: the Palacios Nazaries (Royal Palace), the Generalife gardens and the Alcazaba fortress.
>
> You must enter the palace complex within your allocated half-hour slot, but you can stay as long as you like. If you have to wait, you can visit the Alcazaba at any time, or while away an hour or so in the pleasant cafés and restaurants nearby.
>
> To save the hassle of driving and car-parking, take the Alhambra minibus (marked Conexión Alhambra–Albayzín (Albaicín), every ten minutes from Plaza Nueva). This service also saves the steep climb to the Albaicín, stopping near the San Nicolás mirador.

ⓐ Calle Oficios ⓣ 958 22 92 39 ⓦ www.capillarealgranada.com
ⓛ 10.30–13.00, 16.00–20.00 (summer); 13.30–18.30 (winter)

### Parque de las Ciencias (Science Museum)
This fascinating science museum, which includes a planetarium, has a great range of hands-on multi-media displays and experiments.
ⓐ Avenida del Mediterráneo ⓣ 958 13 19 00 ⓦ www.parqueciencias.com
ⓛ 10.00–19.00 Tues–Sat, 10.00–15.00 Sun ❶ Admission charge

## TAKING A BREAK

**Churreria, Cafeteria Alhambra £ ❶** Of the many popular restaurants set around the lively Plaza Bib-Rambla, this one is hard to beat for greasy but delicious 'churros con chocolate' (akin to a doughnut). For a healthier option, try one of the enormous salads. ⓐ Plaza Bibrambla 27 ⓣ 958 52 39 29 ⓛ 08.00–24.00 (summer); 08.00–22.00 (winter)

## AFTER DARK

### Restaurants

**Parador ££** ❷  The terrace café of Granada's elegant state-owned hotel is less expensive than its formal restaurant, overlooking the Generalife Gardens. ⓐ Real de la Alhambra ❶ 958 22 14 40 ⓦ www.parador.es

**Puerta del Carmen ££** ❸  Granada's well-heeled young couples love this modern new restaurant for its extensive wine list and tempting mix of European and Spanish dishes, right in the centre of town. ⓐ Plaza del Carmen 1 ❶ 958 22 37 37

**Sevilla ££** ❹  Steeped in history, this popular restaurant/tapas bar was the preferred haunt of local writer, García Lorca, and of composer, Manuel de Falla. The 1930s dining room remains unchanged. ⓐ Calle Oficios 12 ❶ 958 22 12 23 ⓦ www.alqueriamorayma.com
🕒 Closed Mon lunch and Sun

**Alhambra Palace Hotel £££** ❺  Come here for an early evening drink to enjoy the brilliant views of the city from the terrace at sunset. ⓐ Calle Peña Partida 2–4 ❶ 958 22 14 68

**Cunini £££** ❻  A traditional favourite in the city centre, specializing in excellent seafood. Tapas are served at the bar, but book ahead for a table. ⓐ Plaza Pescadería 14 ❶ 958 25 07 77 🕒 Closed Mon and Sun eve

**Granero de Abrantes £££** ❼  This stylish place with a high-raftered ceiling has a sophisticated menu (cod with raisins and pine kernels or Alpujarras asparagus soup). Excellent bread. ⓐ Plaza Poeta Luis Rosales, just off the main square ❶ 958 50 80 64

# Mojácar

A dazzling pile of cube-shaped houses scattered on a rocky hilltop, a long beach dotted with palms and spiky agaves cactus – the picture conjured by this *pueblo blanco* in the remotest and most arid part of south-eastern Spain spells Andalucía in bold letters. In a way, the village is an artificial community, recreated by outsiders who 'rediscovered' it during the 1960s and appreciated its distinctive character.

Many of its former inhabitants, debilitated by the Spanish Civil War, had emigrated in search of work and its pretty houses had slid into ruin. An enterprising local mayor encouraged new settlers by offering free plots of building land, and a cosmopolitan colony of artists flocked here in search of an alternative lifestyle. Today, Mojácar is a chic and successful holiday resort that has retained its charm, despite inevitable expansion, to cater for its new visitors. The water is exceptionally clear, and a good range of watersports is available, including diving and fishing. The region is well worth exploring; there are a number of unusual sights and some spectacular scenery nearby. Excursions are organised from the village, but to see the area conveniently, car hire is recommended.

## THINGS TO SEE & DO

### Boat trips
Take a relaxing mini-cruise along the rugged, unspoilt coast. Boats leave daily from Garrucha marina (a short distance to the north) to the Cabo de Gata. ⓐ Puerto Deportivo de Garrucha ❶ 950 46 00 48
**Fishing or dolphin-spotting trips** ⓐ Advertised near the beach, Lolailo Lailo II
Scuba diving with **Mojácar Dive Center** ⓐ Paseo Mediterraneo
❶ 952 47 27 60 Ⓦ www.buceomojacar.com

### Mojácar Pueblo
Most hotels and apartments are down near the beach, but whatever you do, don't miss a chance to explore the old hilltop village 2 km (1 mile)

⏶ *Mojácar is a distinctive sight on a rocky hilltop*

inland. There are no particular sights, but it is one of Andalucía's most charming white towns, full of fascinating little shops and restaurants. The views from its *miradors* (viewing points) are spectacular. Most of its activity centres around the main squares of Plaza Nueva, Plaza de la Iglesia and Plaza del Ayuntamiento.

## Parque Acuático Vera

The local answer to all those Costa del Sol water parks. This one lies near Vera, a little way north of Mojácar.

ⓐ Carretera Vera/Garrucha–Villaricos   ❶ 950 46 73 37

ⓦ www.aquavera.com   ❶ Daily, with seasonal variations

## AFTER DARK

### Restaurants
### Mojácar Beach
The long seafront road has plenty of apartments, shops and eating places, and they are much less oppressive than in many resorts, in simple local styles.

**Bollywood £** Just what it says, offering straightforward, well-cooked curries at good prices. ⓐ Guardia Viega 201 ❶ 950 47 21 14 🕒 Dinner only

**Restaurante El Viento del Desierto £** Very reasonable starters and main courses of the local game. Situated just beside the church.
ⓐ Plaza Frontón ❶ 950 47 86 26 🕒 20.00–23.00

**La Cantina ££** A delightful Mexican-style complex of beachside bar and bistro – nachos and tacos galore. The location is exceptionally good, right by the beach in a shady patch of palms. ⓐ Playa Las Ventanicas
❶ 950 47 88 41 Ⓦ www.lacantinamojacar.com 🕒 Closed Mon off-season; beach bar closed in winter; dinner only

**Lua Pizzeria ££** This is an elegant Italian establishment with very good terrace views over the sea. ⓐ Paseo del Mediterráneo ❶ 950 47 22 24
🕒 Dinner only

### Mojácar Town
**La Cabaña ££** An upmarket Argentinian *parrilla* (barbecue) with an unimpeachable reputation for top notch steaks and gooey grilled cheese.
ⓐ Paseo del Mediterráneo 101 ❶ 950 61 51 79

**Casa Minguito ££** Serves traditional Spanish dishes in a delightful shady square, which doubles as a popular drinking spot at night. ⓐ Plaza Ayuntamiento ❶ 950 47 86 14 🕒 Open daily for lunch and dinner

## THE INDALO

Everywhere around Mojácar you will see a stick-like figure with an arc above its head. This is the Indalo, a symbol found in neolithic cave drawings at nearby **Vélez Blanco**. For centuries, this matchstick man was painted on the doors of local houses to ward off evil and bring good luck to the inhabitants. It is now used as the Costa de Almería's publicity logo.

**Mamabel's ££** A delightful little hotel-restaurant overlooking splendid views. Typical Andalucían-style decor. A shortish but interesting menu, and flamenco on Saturdays. ⓐ Calle Embajadores 5 ⓣ 950 47 24 48 ⓦ www.mamabels.com ⓛ Open for breakfast and dinner

**Palacio ££** A smart little place in the village centre, offering interesting dishes like fresh salmon in prune sauce, or leek cake. ⓐ Plaza del Caño ⓣ 950 47 28 46 ⓛ Dinner only

### Nightlife

A number of open-air discos cater for the small hours on the beach, but many are seasonal and may open only at weekends, except in high summer.

**Badgers ££** Aston Villa fans should make a pilgrimage here. Keith Bradley (an ex-player) runs this lively seafront bar. Plenty of televised football, karaoke and traditional British cooking. ⓐ Paseo del Mediterráneo ⓣ 950 47 85 25

**El Loro Azul ££** Funky jazz bar with legendary *mojitos* (rum and mint cocktail), regular live music and a buzzing atmosphere into the early hours. ⓐ Plaza Frontón ⓛ Eves only, closed Oct–Mar

# Almería

The provincial capital is a town with a very distinguished past, though not much of its former glory survives today. Its Alcazaba, dating from AD 995, was the largest fortress ever built by the Moors in Spain, which gives some idea of what an important place it was. Under the Caliphate of Córdoba, it was a major port for the export of textiles, particularly the silk produced in vast quantities in Las Alpujarras. Gradually, sieges and economic decline took their toll. Today Almería is a dusty little city, extremely poor in places. Its main landmarks, though, are worth a brief visit, and it has some atmospheric, inexpensive tapas bars and nightlife.

## THINGS TO SEE & DO

### Alcazaba (Moorish Castle)

An impressive example of Moorish fortification, this massive castle was badly damaged in an earthquake in 1522. The three separate wards of the fortress and many of the walls are still intact, however, and offer a splendid vantage point over the town and port.

ⓐ Calle Almanzor ⓣ 950 27 16 17 ⓛ 10.00–14.00, 17.00–20.00 Tues–Sun (mid-June–Sept); 09.30–13.30, 15.30–19.00 (Oct–May) ⓘ Free with EU passport

### Cabo de Gata

On the east side of town stretches the hilly cape, which marks Spain's southeastern tip. There's a fine sandy beach here (mainly used by locals), but very little natural shade. This is one of the driest and hottest regions of Spain, and summer temperatures are ferocious. Much of it is a natural park of briny lagoons similar to the ones near Almerimar. Piles of salt are extracted to dry at the southern end. It is visited by flamingos at certain times of year, and there are bird hides to watch them.

### Cathedral

The Gothic cathedral stands on the site of the former mosque, which was destroyed in the earthquake of 1522. Fortified to withstand pirate attack, its exterior is rather plain, but it contains splendid choir stalls and a richly decorated altar in red and black jasper.

📍 Plaza de la Catedral ☎ 609 57 58 02 🕐 10.00–17.30 Mon–Fri, 10.00–13.30 Sat ❶ Admission charge

### Cuevas de Sorbas (Caves of Sorbas)

The extraordinary parched limestone scenery near Sorbas has created some weird formations, notably stalactite caves and deep gorges.

☎ 950 36 47 04 🌐 www.cuevasdesorbas.com 🕐 Different guided tours 10.00–20.00. Telephone to check ❶ Admission charge

### Mini Hollywood

No local excursion programme fails to mention this theme park near Tabernas, north of Almería. There's a fair chance you've already seen it, for this film set and the surrounding desert-like scenery have featured in a number of classic 'spaghetti Westerns', notably the Sergio Leone films that made a big star out of Clint Eastwood, thanks to *A Fistful of Dollars*, *The Good, the Bad and the Ugly* and others. Visitors can wander around the slightly shabby 'town' and watch a cowboy show with plenty of shootings and horsing around. Next to Mini Hollywood is a small zoo (separate entrance charge).

📍 Carretera N340, Km 464 ☎ 950 36 52 36 🕐 Three shows daily: Western, 12.00, 17.00 and 20.00; parrots, 11.00, 15.00 and 18.00; salon dancing, 13.00, 16.00 and 19.00 ❶ Admission charge

### Museum of Almería

Phoenician, Arab and ancient Greek objects discovered by Belgian engineer Louis Siret.

📍 Carretera de Ronda 2/6 ☎ 950 26 44 92

### Níjar

The chief attraction of this pretty village is its handicrafts. The main street is lined with shops selling brightly coloured local pottery, esparto-grass baskets and cheerful, stripy, woven rag rugs or throws called *jarapas*.

## TAKING A BREAK

**Bodega la Aldea £** Tucked away on a little side street, this tiny tapas bar is known for its *surtido la aldea* – a house assortment of cured meats – and the *chalenyer*, a slab of tortilla topped with thick, cold *salmorejo* soup. ⓐ Calle Méndez Nuñez 6 ⓣ 950 25 35 97

**Bodega Montenegro £** Stacked with barrels, a very local traditional *tapas* bar near the cathedral. ⓐ Plaza Granero ⓣ 950 23 30 51

**Cafetería Santa Riba La Rambla ££** Busy boulevard café on one of the main streets. Part of small local chain serving good teas, cakes and *platos combinados* (selection of mixed salads with meats). Tables outside. ⓐ Avenida Estación 2 ⓣ 950 27 19 63

**Casa Puga ££** Bustling local tapas bar with delicious food and fabulous tiled interior. ⓐ Calle Jovellanos 7 ⓣ 950 23 15 30 ⓛ Closed Sun and hols

## AFTER DARK

**Restaurants**
**Restaurante Valentin ££** Smart seafood restaurant with a delicious and tempting menu, in the centre of town. ⓐ Calle Tenor Iribane 2 ⓣ 950 26 44 75 ⓦ www.restaurante-valentin.com

**Restaurante Torreluz Mediterraneo £££** Attached to a four-star hotel, this elegant establishment serves inventive fish and meat dishes, like red mullet stuffed with squid. Save some room for the chocolate mousse with white chocolate sauce and strawberries. ⓐ Plaza Flores 2 ⓣ 950 28 14 25 ⓛ 13.30–16.00, 20.30–23.00, closed Mon eve and Sun

---

❿ *Málaga's busy port*

# Food & drink

From the sophisticated restaurants of Marbella to the simple *chiringuito* (beach bars) of Torremolinos, or the hearty mountain cooking of the *pueblos blancos* (white towns), the cuisine of the Costa del Sol is as wide in variety as it is rich in flavours. For centuries Andalucía has been a land of different cultures, and their influences are reflected in the local food – the Phoenician style of salting, the Roman appreciation of olive oils and garlic, and the Arab taste for sweet dishes, exotic fruits and vegetables. The local cuisine is an ensemble of exotic, spicy dishes and bold, sun-drenched Mediterranean flavours, unique to southern Spain.

## SOUPS
Popular starters include two chilled soups: *gazpacho andaluz* (made with tomato, garlic, sweet peppers and cucumber, and served cold) and *ajo blanco* (made from garlic and almonds, and served with grapes). Try also *sopa de pescado*, a tasty fish soup seasoned with tomato, onion, garlic and brandy, *guisado* made with fish and meat, and *potajes*, thick vegetable soups, which can frequently be found on menus in the mountains.

## FRESH FISH
Fish is the main speciality of the coast. It's fun to lunch on fresh sardines, cooked over a wood fire by local fishermen on the beach. Cheap and tasty, they are usually served with lemon, fresh bread and salad. The daily catch in most resorts includes *bonito* (tuna), *pez espada* (swordfish), *rape* (monkfish), and *lenguado* (sole), all delicious grilled. Also worth a try are *pescaíto frito* (mixed fried fish), *gambas al pil-pil* (prawns sizzling in garlic and chilli), *calamares en su tinta* (squid cooked in its own ink), *risotto à la marinera* (seafood risotto) and, of course, *paella* – a scrumptious rice dish of meat, tomatoes, peppers, onions and seafood.

## MEAT DISHES
Inland, a rich, traditional cuisine incorporates the game and wild herbs of the mountains, with hearty meat dishes including *estofado* (meat stew),

🔺 *Relaxing over a coffee in a shady plaza, Benalmádena*

*fabada* (ham and bean stew), *conejo* (rabbit casserole) and *choto al ajo* (roast kid in garlic sauce). Look out also for *albondigas* (spicy meatballs), *calderetas* (lamb stew with almonds) and one of the most famous Andalucían dishes of all, *rabo de toro* (oxtail, prepared with tomatoes, onions and various spices). Food buffs should sample the many tasty local varieties of sausage and cured ham, up in the hills.

## VEGETARIANS

Vegetarians won't starve in Andalucía. Most menus include a choice of fresh salads, *tortilla* (omelette) and vegetable dishes, such as *garbanzos con espinacas* (chickpeas with spinach), *judías verdes con salsa de tomate* (green beans with tomato sauce) and *pisto de verduras* (ratatouille).

## DESSERTS

Remember to save room for pudding – sweet, sticky *natillas* (cream custards), *yemas del tajo* (based on egg yolks and sugar), *brazo de gitano* (cream-filled pastries) and *piononos* (liqueur-soaked cakes ) or some fresh fruit – oranges, peaches, grapes, raisins, pomegranates and figs – a typical way to round off a meal.

⬢ *Tapas and spices for sale in a local market*

## BRITISH

If you're looking for a taste of home, most resorts can offer fish and chips, steak-and-kidney pie, ploughman's lunches and full English breakfasts, all washed down with a cuppa or a British beer.

## INTERNATIONAL

There are few places in Spain with a greater concentration of restaurants to suit all tastes and budgets than the Costa del Sol. For something hot or spicy, there are Indian, Mexican, Chinese and Indonesian restaurants. If you prefer European, try the numerous French, Italian, German and Swiss restaurants. American fast-food outlets – McDonald's, Pizza Hut, KFC and Burger King – are all here as well.

## TAPAS

This area of Spain is well known for tapas, small snacks served with drinks in most cafés and bars. The food is usually displayed on the bar so you can order it simply by pointing. The variety is endless – smoked ham, spicy sausage, cheese, olives, sardines, mushrooms, prawns, mussels, squid, octopus, anchovies, etc. They are served in small portions, which allow you to sample several different dishes at once. Or you can follow the Andalucían custom of moving from bar to bar, sampling just one dish in each – a kind of Spanish-style pub-crawl!

## DRINKS

Spanish wine is the perfect accompaniment for such a rich assortment of dishes, so be sure to try the sweet wines of Málaga. However, many Spaniards prefer beer, such as Cruzcampo and San Miguel.

Sherry is a popular tapas accompaniment. There are many different types to choose from, including *fino* (light, dry and pale yellow), *manzanilla* (dry and delicate), *oloroso* (sweet, dark and full-bodied) or *amontillado* (amber and medium-dry).

A favourite drink worth trying is *sangría* – a jug of red wine, rum or brandy, fruit and lemonade, served chilled with ice. Or, for a special treat, try white *sangría*, made with sparkling white wine.

# Menu decoder

**aceitunas aliñadas** Marinated olives

**albóndigas de pescado** Fish cakes

**albóndigas en salsa** Meatballs in (usually tomato) sauce

**alioli** Garlic-flavoured mayonnaise served as an accompaniment to just about anything

**bistec or biftek** Beef steak; rare is *poco hecho*, medium is *regular* and well done is *muy hecho* (ask for it more well cooked than at home)

**bocadillo** The Spanish sandwich, usually made of French-style bread

**caldereta** A stew based on fish or lamb

**caldo** A soup or broth

**carne** Meat; *carne de ternera* is beef; *carne picada* is minced meat; *carne de cerdo* is pork; *carne de cordero* is lamb

**chorizo** A cured, dry, red-coloured sausage made from chopped pork, paprika, spices, herbs and garlic

**churros** Flour fritters cooked in spiral shapes in very hot fat and cut into strips, best dunked into hot chocolate

**cordero asado** Roast lamb flavoured with lemon and white wine

**embutidos charcutería** Pork meat preparations including *jamón* (ham), *chorizo* (see above), *salchichones* (sausages) and *morcillas* (black pudding)

**ensalada** Salad; the normal restaurant salad is composed of lettuce, onion, tomato and olives

**ensalada mixta** As above, but with extra ingredients, such as boiled egg, tuna fish or asparagus

**escabeche** A sauce of fish, meat or vegetables cooked in wine and vinegar and left to go cold

**estofado de buey** Beef stew made with carrots and turnips, or with potatoes

**fiambre** Any type of cold meat such as ham, chorizo, etc

**flan** Caramel custard, the national dessert of Spain

**fritura** A fry-up, as in *fritura de pescado* – different kinds of fried fish

**gambas** Prawns; *gambas a la plancha* are grilled, *gambas al ajillo* are fried with garlic and *gambas con gabardina* are deep fried in batter

**gazpacho andaluz** Cold soup (originally from Andalucía) made from tomatoes, cucumbers, peppers, garlic and olive oil

**gazpacho manchego** (Not to be confused with *gazpacho andaluz*) a hot dish made with meat (chicken or rabbit) and unleavened bread

**habas con jamón** Broad beans fried with diced ham (sometimes with chopped hard boiled egg and parsley)

**helado** Ice cream

**jamón** Ham; *jamón serrano* and *jamón iberico* (far more expensive) are dry cured; cooked ham is *jamón de york*

**langostinos a la plancha** Large prawns grilled and served with *alioli* or vinaigrette; *langostinos a la marinera* are cooked in white wine

**lenguado** Sole, often served cooked with wine and mushrooms

**mariscos** shellfish

**menestra** A dish of mixed vegetables cooked separately and combined before serving

**menú del día** Set menu for the day at a fixed price; it may or may not include bread, wine and a dessert, but it doesn't usually include coffee

**paella** Famous rice dish originally from Valencia but now made all over Spain; *paella valenciana* has chicken and rabbit; *paella de mariscos* is made with

seafood; *paella mixta* combines meat and seafood

**pan** Bread; *pan de molde* is sliced white bread; wholemeal is *pan integral*

**pincho moruno** Pork kebab: spicy chunks of pork on a skewer

**pisto** The Spanish version of ratatouille, made with tomato, peppers, onions, garlic, courgettes and aubergines

**pollo al ajillo** Chicken fried with garlic; *pollo a la cerveza* is cooked in beer; *pollo al chilindrón* is cooked with peppers, tomatoes and onions

**salpicón de mariscos** Seafood salad

**sopa de ajo** Delicious, warming, winter garlic soup thickened with bread, usually with a poached egg floating in it

**tarta helada** A popular ice cream cake served as dessert

**tortilla de patatas** The classic omelette, also called *tortilla española*, made with potatoes; it can be eaten hot or cold; if you want a plain omelette ask for a *tortilla francesa*

**zarzuela de pescado y mariscos** A stew made with white fish and shellfish in a tomato, wine and saffron stock

LIFESTYLE

⬥ *Shaded from the blistering sun, the main shopping street in Málaga*

# Shopping

Shopping is one of the favourite pastimes for visitors to the Costa del Sol, with a huge range of items to buy and places to buy them.

## MARKETS

Bargain hunters will love the hustle and bustle of the local markets. The best buys are fruit and vegetables, leather goods, ceramics and lace. Don't forget to barter, this is very normal at markets in Spain, so you won't be offending anyone – it's also great fun. Most major resorts along the coast have a morning market once a week. Fuengirola Market (Tues) has the reputation of being the biggest, cheapest and best, while the market in Nerja (Tues) is noted for its charm and atmosphere.

## GIFTS & HANDICRAFTS

The best holiday buys here are local handicrafts, including lace, colourful ceramics, and attractive basketwork. You will find plenty of choice in the craft shops of Ronda, Mijas and other mountain villages. For shoes, handbags, belts and wallets, head to Córdoba, famous for its leather and also its filigree silverware. Granada is well known for its inlaid woodwork (such as music boxes and chess boards) while good buys in Sevilla include embroidered shawls and ceramics.

## FASHIONS

Marbella and central Málaga are probably the best places for clothes shopping, with their chic boutiques and fashion stores. For trendy designer boutiques and a glamorous backdrop of millionaires' yachts, Puerto Banús is every shopper's paradise, even just for window-shopping. More affordable, and one of the best shopping streets on the coast, is Torremolinos' Calle San Miguel, where you can find just about anything from leather goods to Lladró porcelain. The Costa del Sol is also a good place to buy sports clothing and equipment, especially at the end of the season. Mojácar is a good place to buy souvenirs and presents.

# Children

There is plenty to amuse children on the Costa del Sol. Apart from the obvious pleasures of the beach or hotel pool, the area has many attractions aimed at entertaining youngsters of all ages. Many of the hotels organise children's programmes of fun, games and outings, and the tourist offices have lists of all the local attractions geared towards children.

## ANIMAL MAGIC
There are a whole host of animal-orientated activities along the coast, which are fun for children, including the Fuengirola Zoo (see page 31), the Crocodile Park and the spectacular shows of Andalucían horse dressage at El Ranchito both near Torremolinos (see page 44).

## BOAT TRIPS
Older children will relish the idea of a boat excursion to explore the coastline. Most resorts offer trips, some include opportunities for swimming, diving and snorkelling, too.

## FAMILY RESTAURANTS
Spaniards adore children, which means they are welcome almost everywhere, notably in restaurants (even late at night). Some have high chairs available and most have children's choices on the menu. If not, just ask, and the restaurant is more than likely to offer child-size portions.

## MINI-TRAINS
Most resorts have a mini-train, enabling parents to see the sights while keeping the kids happy.

## SPORTS
When the family has tired of the beach, why not have a quick round of mini-golf, take them horse riding or, for an exciting afternoon, try a few circuits of go-karting.

🔺 *Mini-train: see the sights and keep the kids happy*

## TIVOLI WORLD

There are lots of thrills and great entertainment to be had in the Tivoli wonderland, the largest amusement park on the Costa (see page 39). Kids can have a go on all their favourite fairground rides like the waltzers, the big wheel, the ghost train and the dodgems, as well as seeing some traditional flamenco, Western or circus shows – a great day out for children young and old.

## WATER FUN PARKS

A splashing time is guaranteed for all the family at the Aquapark, Torremolinos (see page 43) and the Parque Aquático de Mijas (see page 32), with a variety of activities including the largest water-slide in Europe, wave machines, rapids and a mini aquatic park for small children.

LIFESTYLE

# Sports & activities

### CYCLING

Cycling and mountain biking are excellent ways to enjoy the Andalucían countryside. The tourist board has a guide covering 120 itineraries, with maps, hill profiles, time required and difficulty ratings available from most tourist information offices. Two reliable bike-hire shops are:

**Motomercado** ⓐ Avda Jesús Santos Rein 47, Los Boliches, Fuengirola ⓣ 952 47 25 51 ⓦ www.rentabike.org and **Xtrem Bike** ⓐ Las Mercedes 14, Torremolinos ⓣ 952 38 06 91

### GOLF

The Costa del Sol is often called the Costa del Golf, and not without reason. With 40-plus courses within just 120 km (75 miles) of coastline, it is Europe's number-one winter golf destination, with some of the finest courses in the world. Most courses demand a handicap certificate and in high season (Jan–May, Sept–Nov), book tee-times well in advance.

**La Dama de Noche**  A 9-hole course, offers floodlit golf, enabling tee off as late as 22.00 ⓐ Camino del Angel, Marbella ⓣ 952 81 81 50

**Los Arqueros Golf**  Founded by world-champion Manuel Pinero – tuition at all levels. ⓐ Carretera de Ronda, Km 42.9 ⓣ 952 78 46 00

**Marbella Golf and Country Club** ⓐ Carretera N340, Km 187 ⓣ 952 83 05 00

**Mijas Golf** ⓐ Carretera Coín, Km 3 ⓣ 952 47 68 43

**Sotogrande** ⓐ Carretera N340, Km 130 ⓣ 956 78 50 14

**Valderrama**  Setting of the 1997 Ryder Cup. ⓐ Carretera N340, Km 132 ⓣ 956 79 12 00

### HORSE RIDING

**Centre Hípico Hoppla** outside Mijas offers horse rental and excursions. ⓐ Calle Enterrios 49, Mijas Costa ⓣ 952 11 90 74

**Lakeview Equestrian Centre** in San Pedro organises treks in the countryside. ⓐ Urbanisacion Valle del Sol, San Pedro ⓣ 952 78 69 34

## JEEP SAFARIS

Discover rural Spain by jeep with **Marbella Rangers** 🕿 952 83 30 82 or **Niza Cars** of Torremolinos 🕿 952 38 14 48

## SCUBA-DIVING

Nerja's crystal-clear water is a good place for beginners. Useful contacts include: **Aquatech** 🕿 952 66 03 27 in Fuengirola; **Club de Buceo** 🕿 952 56 23 65 in Benalmádena and **Club Náutique** 🕿 952 52 46 54 in Nerja

## SKIING

North-east of Nerja, the Sierra Nevada is the most southerly ski region in Europe and one of the highest. Its most popular ski resort is just 31 km (19 miles) from Granada. **Solynieve** 🕿 958 24 91 00 🌐 www.skireport.com/spain for ski reports

## TENNIS

Many resort hotels have tennis courts, and many clubs organise regular summer tournaments and other programmes. Among the smartest are: **Club de Tenis Lew Hoad** 🅐 Carretera de Mijas Km 3.5 🕿 952 47 48 58 **Hotel Puente Romano** 🅐 Carretera de Cadiz Km 177 🕿 952 82 09 00

## WATERSKIING

Waterskiing is available from most marinas and also at **Funny Beach**, the watersports centre just east of Marbella 🅐 Carretera N340, Km 184 🕿 952 82 33 59 🌐 www.funnybeach.net. Alternatively, **Cable Ski Marbella** offers the perfect way for beginners to learn – in calm waters and without a boat! Instead, an overhead cable takes you round an 800 m ($\frac{1}{2}$ mile) circuit 🅐 Guadalmina Alta, Parque de las Madrana, 29 670 Pedro de Alcantera 🕿 952 78 55 79 🌐 www.marbellacableski.com

## WINDSURFING & KITESURFING

The main windsurfing/kitesurfing season runs from March to November here. Just beyond Gibraltar, Tarifa is the windsurfing capital of Europe, just 14 km (9 miles) from the coast of North Africa.

# Festivals & events

## FESTIVALS

Every town has a *feria* (festival) to celebrate their patron saint's day and these festivals usually involve lively parades, music, dancing, food, wine, street processions and sometimes bull-fights, funfairs and circuses. At night, vast paellas are cooked over an open fire and the celebrations continue with singing, flamenco and fireworks. The largest and most spectacular is in Málaga in August. For more details consult
Ⓦ www.andalucia.com/festival

## FLAMENCO

Flamenco originates from Andalucía, with Moorish origins that can be heard in the dance's wailing chants. There are two types of flamenco – the slow, emotional *Cante Jondo* (deep song) and the bright, cheerful *Cante Chico* (light song), with rousing melodies and, of course, the wonderful, rhythmic clapping, stamping and castanet playing. With the men in their slim, Córdoban suits and the women in sweeping, ruffled gypsy dresses, the dance offers excitement and colour second to none:

**Ali Oli** ⓐ Paseo Marítimo, Fuengirola ⓣ 952 19 93 19 Ⓛ Fri nights

**Los Gallos** ⓐ Plaza de Santa Cruz, Sevilla ⓣ 954 21 69 81 Ⓛ Nightly at 21.00 and 23.30

**Pepe Lopez** ⓐ Plaza de la Gamba Alegre, Torremolinos ⓣ 952 38 12 84 Ⓛ Mon–Sat nights

**Sala Flamenca Donde Maña** ⓐ Calle Vicente Blasco, Marbella ⓣ 654 68 55 75 Ⓛ Mon–Sat at 23.00

**Tablao Cardenal** ⓐ Calle Torrijos, Córdoba 10 ⓣ 957 48 31 12 Ⓛ Wed–Sun at 22.30

The mesmerising excitement of a flamenco display

⬤ *Colourful boats adorn the beaches*

### VIRGEN DEL CARMEN

If you happen to take a holiday on the Costa del Sol on 16 July, you should make an effort to catch this colourful and lively fiesta. Essentially, it's a 'blessing of the waters' ceremony, a reminder that those big holiday resorts were once just simple fishing communities. There are several days of events, which culminate in a splendid procession in which the patron saint of fishermen is carried from the church into the sea. The celebrations take place in several places, but are especially magnificent in **Los Boliches, Fuengirola**.

◗ *The picturesque mountain roads of Andalucía*

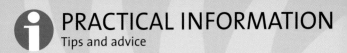

# PRACTICAL INFORMATION
Tips and advice

# Accommodation

Hotels below are graded by approximate price:
£ = budget   ££ = mid-range   £££ = expensive

### AGUADULCE
**Hotel Playadulce ££** A comfortable hotel in Aguadulce's tourist centre, with a buffet restaurant, swimming pool and tennis courts. Officially 4-star, but feels more like 3. ⓐ Paseo del Palmreal ⓣ 950 34 12 74

### ALMERIMAR
**Almerimar Hotel El Ejido ££** Tiered modern block facing the sea on one side and an 18-hole golf course on the other. Fully equipped with tennis courts, squash courts, swimming pool, hairdresser, nightly entertainment and crèche. One of very few hotels in this upmarket development.
ⓐ Avenida de Almerimar, Almerimar ⓣ 950 49 70 07
ⓦ www.hotel-almerimar.com

### BENALMADENA COSTA
**Sunset Beach Club ££** Good value holiday hotel set away from the Puerto Deportivo, close to a good beach the far side of Castillo Bil-Bil.
ⓐ Avenida del Sol 5, Benalmadena Costa ⓣ 952 57 94 00
ⓦ www.sunsetbeachclub.com

### ESTEPONA
**Hotel Mediterráneo £** Simple 1-star hotel facing the sea and a short walk from Estepona's old town centre. Recommended budget option.
ⓐ Avenida de España 68 ⓣ 952 79 33 93

### FUENGIROLA
**Hostal Marbella £** Quaint little family-run hotel in one of the nicest streets in Fuengirola town centre, and a short walk from the beach.
ⓐ Calle Marbella 34, Fuengirola ⓣ 952 66 45 03
ⓦ www.hostalmarbellainfo/en/index.php

## MARBELLA

**Hotel los Monteros £££** One of Marbella's premier hotels, this deluxe 5-star hotel has a renowned haute cuisine restaurant and a private beach club. ⓐ Carretera Cádiz, Km 187 ⓣ 952 77 17 00 ⓦ www.monteros.com

## NERJA

**Hotel Nerja Princess ££** Small hotel in Nerja town centre, five minutes from the sea and the Balcón de Europa. Facilities include a swimming pool. ⓐ Calle Los Huertos 64, Nerja ⓣ 952 52 89 86 ⓦ www.hotelnp.com

## PUERTO BANÚS

**Hotel H10 Andalucia Plaza £££** Plush 4-star hotel, with swimming pool, Turkish baths, casino and two different restaurants in one of the most upmarket districts on the Costa del Sol. ⓐ Urbanisacion Nueva Andalucía, Puerto Banús ⓣ 952 24 32 42

## ROQUETAS

**Aparthotel Fenix £** German-run establishment aimed at guests staying a week or more. Each room comes with a kitchenette, dining area and balcony, and there is a weekly maid service and a shady pool. ⓐ Calle Alameda ⓣ 950 33 34 10

## SAN PEDRO DE ALCÁNTARA

**Hotel El Cortijo Blanco ££** Mid-range alternative to the sky-rise blocks that dominate further up the coast, with sensitive architecture, simple Andalucían furnishings and an outdoor swimming pool. ⓐ Avenida Jose Luis Carrillo Benitez, San Pedro de Alcántara ⓣ 952 78 90 00

## TORREMOLINOS

**Hotel los Jazmines ££** Towerblock hotel with its own swimming pool and gardens, a good walk from Torremolinos town but just across the road from the beach and a number of good *chiringuitos* (beachbars) ⓐ Avenida del Lido 6, Torremolinos ⓣ 952 38 50 33 ⓦ www.hotellosjazmines.com

# Preparing to go

## GETTING THERE

The Costa del Sol and the Costa de Almería are easily reached by plane, with regular flights direct to Málaga, Almería, Sevilla, Jerez, Granada and Gibraltar by British Airways, Monarch and Iberia (the Spanish national airline), as well as budget carriers such as Ryanair and easyJet. The websites www.opodo.co.uk and www.expedia.co.uk are useful for tracking down the cheapest deals.

In July and August, when prices tend to rise considerably, package holidays may offer the best value. If your travelling times are flexible, and you can avoid the school holidays, look for cheap last-minute deals on websites such as www.lastminute.co.uk or in papers like the *Economist*, the *Sunday Telegraph*, *The Sunday Times* and the *Mail on Sunday* .

Alternatively you can travel by ferry, which may work out to be cheaper and more convenient for families taking their own car. There is a 29-hour trip from Portsmouth to Bilbao with P&O or a 19-hour crossing from Plymouth to Santander with Brittany Ferries.

**British Airways** ❶ 0870 850 9850 Ⓦ www.ba.com
**Brittany Ferries** ❶ 08709 076 103 Ⓦ www.brittany-ferries.co.uk
**easyJet** ❶ 0905 821 0905 (premium rate number) Ⓦ www.easyjet.com
**Iberia** ❶ 0845 6012854 Ⓦ www.iberiaairlines.co.uk
**Interrail** ❶ 08700 841 410 Ⓦ www.interrail.com
**Monarch** ❶ 08700 405 040 Ⓦ www.flymonarch.com
**P&O Ferries** ❶ 08705 980 333 Ⓦ www.poferries.com
**Ryanair** ❶ 08712 460 000 (Great Britain) or 0818 303 030 (Ireland)
Ⓦ www.ryanair.com

Many people are aware that air travel emits $CO_2$, which contributes to climate change. You may be interested in the possibility of lessening the environmental impact of your flight through the charity Climate Care, which offsets your $CO_2$ by funding environmental projects around the world. Visit Ⓦ www.climatecare.org

## INSURANCE

Have you got sufficient cover for your holiday? Check that your policy covers you adequately for loss of possessions and valuables, for activities you might want to try – such as scuba-diving, horse riding, or watersports – and for emergency medical and dental treatment, including flights home if required.

The EHIC card replaced the old E111 form and entitles British citizens to reduced-cost and sometimes free state-provided medical treatment in the EEA. For further information, ring the EHIC enquiries line: 0845 605 0707 or visit www.ehicard.org

## TOURISM AUTHORITY

Contact the Spanish National Tourist Office ⓐ 22–23 Manchester Square, London W1M 5AP ⓣ 020 7486 8077. It is best to write or visit in person, or you can consult the Spanish National Tourist Office website at www.tourspain.co.uk

For information about Gibraltar, contact the Gibraltar Information Bureau ⓐ Arundel Great Court, 179 Strand, London WC2R 1EH ⓣ 020 7836 0777 ⓦ www.gibraltar.gov.uk

Another useful site dedicated to living and holidaying in southern Spain is www.andalucia.com, whilst www.visitcostadelsol.com deals specifically with the Costa del Sol.

## BEFORE YOU LEAVE

It is not necessary to have inoculations to travel in Europe, but make sure you and your family are up to date with the basics, such as tetanus. It is a good idea to pack a well-stocked first-aid kit. Sun lotion can be more expensive than in the UK so it is worth taking a good selection. Take enough of your prescription medicines with you – they may be difficult to obtain in Spain. It is also worth having a dental check-up before you travel.

## ENTRY FORMALITIES

The most important documents you will need are your tickets and your passport. Check well in advance that your passport is up to date and has at least three months left to run. All children, including newborn babies, need their own passport unless they are already included on the passport of the person they are travelling with. It generally takes at least three weeks to process a passport renewal. For the latest information, contact the **Passport Agency** (☎ 0870 521 0410 ⓦ www.ukpa.gov.uk). Citizens of the UK, Ireland, other EU countries, the US, Canada, Australia and New Zealand do not require a visa for stays of up to 90 days. Citizens of South Africa will need to apply in advance for a Schengen visa, which permits entry into Spain and other Schengen countries for 90 days in each six-month period.

## MONEY

Spain uses the euro (€), available in 500, 200, 100, 50, 20, 10 and 5 euro notes and 2 and 1 euro coins. Many shops do not accept 500 and 200 euro notes because of the risk of counterfeit currency. In winter most banks open 08.30–14.00 Monday to Friday and until 12.00 on Saturday, although these hours may vary slightly from branch to branch. Summer hours are shorter, usually 08.30 until 13.30 or 14.00. For foreign exchange, look out for the sign *Cambio*. These are generally open seven days a week 10.00–21.00, but hours vary widely.

All major credit cards are widely accepted, but cash is preferred for smaller purchases and in more rural areas. Holders of Visa and MasterCard can use the plentiful 24-hour automatic cash dispensers (ATMs), which have instructions in English. There are ATMs at all Spanish airports, but it can be a good idea to get hold of some euros from your local bank or the bureau de change at your departure airport to save you the hassle of hunting one down when you arrive.

The safest way to carry large amounts of money is as traveller's cheques (which are refunded in the event that they are lost or stolen) or to withdraw cash directly from your account as you go using ATMs. Most UK banks charge a minimum fee for overseas withdrawals, so it is cheaper to withdraw a few large amounts than lots of small ones. Before you go, contact your card providers and let them know you will be travelling to Spain; otherwise they may assume your card details have been stolen and suspend your account. If you use your debit or credit cards to pay for things directly, be aware that you may be asked to validate purchases with a signature *and* your pin code. Many shops also request a passport as proof of identity.

## CLIMATE

The Costa del Sol and the Costa de Almería are reliably sunny all year round, but are at their best for beach holidays from the beginning of June to the end of August, when average temperatures range from 28°C (82°F) to 40°C (104°F) and there is very little rainfall. However, inland destinations can be unbearably hot at this time of year. With no sea breeze to cool things down in Sevilla and Córdoba, in August the mercury zooms well over 40°C (104°F). The region is much less busy in spring and autumn, and these can be lovely seasons to visit, with temperatures regularly climbing into the twenties but still cool enough to sightsee and sit out in the sun without burning. The winter sees a bit more rain and will often demand a coat, but the weather is still relatively mild, with average temperatures from 8°C (46°F) to 17°C (63°F).

## BAGGAGE ALLOWANCE

Baggage allowances vary according to the airline, destination and the class of travel, but most airlines allow each passenger to take one piece of luggage weighing up to 20 kg (44 lb) to be carried in the hold. You are also allowed one item of cabin baggage weighing no more than 5 kg (11 lb), and measuring 55 x 40 x 20 cm (22 x 16 x 8 in). Under current security rules, a woman's handbag counts as the item of cabin baggage; you may only carry liquids on board if each product is less than 100ml (3½ fl oz) and they are carried separately in a see-through bag. Large items – surfboards, golf-clubs, skis, collapsible wheelchairs and pushchairs – are usually charged as extras and it is a good idea to let the airline know in advance if you want to bring these.

# During your stay

## AIRPORTS

**Almería** Car hire and taxis are both readily available, or take the airport shuttle bus (06.35 to 22.35, every 20 minutes Mon–Fri, or 40 minutes Sat–Sun) to Almería centre for connections to Aguadulce, Almerimar, Roquettas del Mar, Mojácar, Sevilla, Córdoba and other destinations.

**Gibraltar** This tiny airport is well placed for visiting the western edge of the Costa del Sol, and will be even better suited by mid-2008 when a new terminal is constructed with a direct exit to Spain. The expansion plans will also see a boost to the number of flights and services. There are always taxis in front of the building to take you into Gibraltar or across the border. A Portillo bus runs from the terminal in La Línea to Málaga, making a number of coastal stops.

**Granada-Jaén** Officially Federico García Lorca Airport, this growing facility is located 16 km (10 miles) west of Granada near the small town of Santa Fé. Buses run to Granada city roughly every two hours, from 09.05 to 23.00, and car rental and taxis are available.

**Jerez** Full car-hire facilities and taxis to local destinations. Daily buses run to Ronda, La Línea (for Gibraltar), Marbella and Málaga – a five-hour journey.

**Málaga Airport** is located 8 km (5 miles) southwest of Málaga city and is by far the Costa del Sol's busiest airport. All major car hire companies are represented and taxis are available from just outside the arrivals hall. Public transport connections are also good: buses run every half hour from 06.30–23.30 to the main bus terminal in Málaga city, where there are connections to Estepona, Fuengirola, Mijas, La Linea (for Gibraltar) and Ronda, and throughout the region. Direct buses run between the airport and Marbella, every 45 minutes between 06.15 and 23.45. There is also an excellent train service between Málaga city, via the airport and on to Fuengirola, Torremolinos and Arroyo de la Miel, which operates every 30 minutes (06.45 to 23.00) and takes about 40 minutes.

**Sevilla** Located about 10 km (6 miles) northwest of Sevilla and about three hours' drive from Málaga, this airport is well served by car hire companies and rail links to Málaga as well as Madrid and Algeciras (just east of Gibraltar).

## COMMUNICATIONS

### Telephones

Public telephones in Spain are easy to use and easy to spot – mounted on posts or in glazed, silver *cabinas telefónicas* (phone booths). They accept coins and/or phone cards, which can be purchased at news-stands and *estancos* (tobacconists), and many of them also have a button that you can press for instructions in English. Most have a list of international dialling codes, and useful numbers like the operator (1004) and directory services (1003).

### Postal services

Postboxes are bright yellow and can be found at railway stations and post offices (*correos*) as well as dotted around town. Stamps (*sellos*) can be bought from *correos* (post offices) or *estancos* (tobacconists). The postal service itself is renowned for being slow and unreliable, with postcards to Europe taking a month to arrive because post boxes are sometimes not emptied for days. For the most reliable service, post letters at the post office itself or use *certificado* (registered) and *urgente* (express) mail. Main post offices are open 08.30–20.30 Mon–Fri, 09.30–14.00 Sat.

### Internet access

Internet cafés are readily available in the big tourist centres but can be hard to find in smaller towns or off the beaten track.

> ### TELEPHONING SPAIN
>
> To call Spain from abroad, dial **00** (the international access code), then the country code (**34**), then the area code (minus the initial **0**), then the number. The country code for Gibraltar is **35**.
>
> #### Telephoning Abroad
>
> The country code for the UK is **44**; for the Republic of Ireland **353**; for the US and Canada **1**; for Australia **61**; for New Zealand **64**; and for South Africa **27**.

## DRESS CODES

Dress codes in Spain are pretty relaxed. Spanish men tend to wear short-sleeved, collared shirts or polo shirts, but T-shirts are just as acceptable. Women, meanwhile, have a love affair with lycra, and small, strappy tops are de rigeur for the young – usually teamed with heels and big earrings. Slightly older women go in for tailoring and are a little more covered up, with grooming high on the agenda. Both men and women dress up a bit more in the evening and also to attend church. Topless sun bathing is acceptable on beaches away from town centres, but locals don't take too kindly to tourists wearing beach clothes in town, so be sensitive to this and cover up, even if others don't.

## ELECTRICITY

The current in Spain is 220 V with two-pin, round-pronged plugs. Adaptors can be found in many hypermarkets, supermarkets and also some electrical stores. If you can, take one with you to be on the safe side. Most hotels and *pensiones* have sockets for hairdryers and shavers in the bedrooms. If you are considering buying electrical appliances to take home, always check that they will work in your country before you buy.

## GETTING AROUND

### Car hire and driving

As well as international car hire companies, a few Spanish companies, such as Atesa, operate nationwide. You can probably negotiate the best deal with an international company from home. There are car hire desks at airports and offices in the large towns. Alternatively, if you wish to hire a car locally for, say, a week or less, you can arrange it with a local travel agent. A car for hire is called a *coche de alquiler*. Car hire prices and conditions vary according to the region and locality. To hire a car in Spain you need show only a current driving licence.

If you take your own car to Spain, you don't need any special documentation but make sure you have all the relevant papers from your country of origin: your driving licence, vehicle registration document and insurance. Your insurance company should be able to arrange an

## EMERGENCIES

For urgent police, fire or ambulance assistance, dial 112.

**Medical emergencies** In case of a medical emergency, head to the nearest *Urgencias* – the emergency ward of a hospital or clinic. The Costa del Sol has a hospital with English-speaking staff situated on the main coastal highway (N340) just east of Marbella (Hospital Costa del Sol, Carretera Nacional N340, Km 187, Marbella, Málaga). All cities have at least one hospital, and most have volunteer interpreters who speak English and occasionally also other languages.

If you need to use your EHIC Card, do not part with the original but hand over a photocopy instead. If you have private travel insurance, make sure you have your policy on you when requesting medical assistance. Depending on the insurance company, you may be expected to pay for treatment and be reimbursed at a later date.

For minor emergencies, staff at *farmacias* (chemists) will be able to suggest remedies for medical problems. They are open 09.30–13.30, 17.00–20.30 Monday to Friday, and are easily recognised by a large green or red cross. After these times and on Saturdays and Sundays, there will always be a duty chemist open, details of which will be posted on every chemist's window.

### Police

There are three types of police in Spain: the *Guardia Civil*, the *Policía Nacional* and the *Policía Local*. The *Policía Nacional*, who wear a blue uniform, are the best to turn to when reporting a crime. When approaching them, remember that it is illegal to be without ID.

### Consulates

The British Consulate is at Plaza Nueva 87, 41001 Sevilla ☎ 954 22 88 74 and Calle Mauricio Moro Pareto, 2 Málaga ☎ 952 35 23 00.

overseas extension of your car insurance. When driving from Britain, if you have an old-style green licence you will need to purchase an International Driving Permit, obtained from the RAC or the AA.

In Spain people drive on the right, so you must give way to the right. At roundabouts, you should give way to cars already on the roundabout but be extremely careful when on a roundabout yourself: do not expect oncoming cars to stop. Some will disregard you and drive straight on.

The speed limits are 50 km/h (30 mph) in built-up areas; 90–100 km/h (55–60 mph) outside them and 120 km/h (75 mph) on motorways. Seatbelts are compulsory for the drivers and passengers in the back and front; motor cyclists must wear crash helmets. Drivers must carry two warning triangles and can be fined by the traffic police for not being equipped with a first-aid kit.

### Taxis

These are essential for access to out-of-town nightspots. Drivers rarely speak any English, so learn enough Spanish to explain where you are going and to negotiate the fare. The meter marks up the basic fare; however, supplements may be added for *tarifa nocturna* (night driving), *maletas* (luggage), or *dias festivos* (public holidays).

### Public transport

**Buses** Buses run frequently (every 20–30 minutes) within and between resorts and are reasonably priced. You usually buy your ticket from the driver or you can buy strips of ten tickets called *bonobus* from *estancos* (tobacconists) and stationers. It is not unusual for buses to be crowded.

**Trains** An excellent train service, with air-conditioning and announcements in Spanish and English, runs between Málaga and Fuengirola, stopping at the airport, Torremolinos and Arroyo de la Miel.

## HEALTH, SAFETY AND CRIME

Pickpockets are common in crowded areas, especially outside monuments and at markets. Be particularly wary of people asking you the time, as they are probably trying to distract you while someone else attempts to snatch your bag or wallet. Use traveller's cheques, eurocheques or credit cards rather than cash, and carry a photocopy of your passport, leaving the original in the hotel safe. In the event of being robbed or attacked, try to report the incident to the police as soon as possible (at least within 24 hours). This is extremely important if you wish to obtain a statement (*denuncia*) to make an insurance claim.

The abundance of street life means that you will rarely find yourself alone or in a position to be harassed. However, women may be intimidated by men passing comment as they walk by, or even following them. This pastime, known as *piropo*, is common and not meant as a serious threat.

The biggest danger you are likely to face is overexposure to the sun, particularly from May to October when temperatures can reach up to 45°C (113°F). Try to avoid walking in the midday sun and stay in the shade whenever possible. Drink plenty of bottled mineral water. It is advisable to wear sunglasses and a hat when you are out sightseeing.

It is a good idea to stick to bottled water at all times, especially in the summer when the river beds dry up and cause pollutants in the water system to become concentrated. Food in Spain is as reliable as anywhere else in Europe.

## OPENING HOURS

**Banks** Open for business from 08.30 to 14.00 Monday to Friday, and from 08.30 to 13.00 on Saturdays during the winter. Banks are never open on public holidays, and during a town's annual *feria* week they open from 09.00 to 12.00.

**Churches** Most churches open only for Mass but in small towns a caretaker will often let visitors in between religious services. Mass is held every hour on Sundays, and at about 19.00–21.00 on weekdays. Dress codes are not as strict as in other Catholic countries but avoid skimpy shorts and bare arms.

**Museums** Hours kept by monuments and museums vary considerably so it is best to check before you visit. Most close on Sunday afternoons. However, during the tourist season many museums stay open all day.

**Shops** Spanish shops tend to close during the afternoon siesta (except for department stores, shopping malls and touristy souvenir shops in the large towns). Most shops open at 09.30 and close at 13.30. They usually reopen about 17.00 or 17.30 and stay open until 20.30 or 21.00.

## RELIGION
Spain is predominantly Catholic.

## TIME DIFFERENCES
Spain is one hour ahead of Greenwich Mean Time (GMT) and British Summer Time.

## TIPPING
Tipping tends to be an issue of discretion in Spain. A service charge (*servicio*) is usually included in bills, but it is common to tip up to 10 per cent in addition and to give small change to petrol pump attendants, taxi drivers, porters and parking attendants.

## TOILETS
Public toilets are scarce, but there is a bar on virtually every corner, which is legally bound to allow you to use their toilets. Nevertheless some bars do so reluctantly if no purchase has been made. A 'D' on the door stands for *Damas* (ladies), and a 'C' indicates *Caballeros* (men).

## TRAVELLERS WITH DISABILITIES
Modern buildings generally have adequate provision for the disabled, with lifts, ramps and toilet facilities. However, owing to their construction, entry to certain historical monuments may be restricted. Local tourist offices, or the monument staff, can provide information about wheelchair access.